WHEN DOING ISN'T ENOUGH

waiting is plenty

WHEN DOING ISN'T ENOUGH

Mary Detweiler

When Doing Isn't Enough
Copyright © 2015 by Mary Detweiler. All rights reserved.

No part of this publication may be reproduced, stored in a retrieval system or transmitted in any way by any means, electronic, mechanical, photocopy, recording or otherwise without the prior permission of the author except as provided by USA copyright law.

Unless otherwise indicated, all Scripture quotations are taken from the Holy Bible, New Living Translation, copyright © 1996. Used by permission of Tyndale House Publishers, Inc., Wheaton, Illinois 60189. All rights reserved.

Scripture quotations marked (MSG) are taken from *TheMessage*. Copyright © 1993, 1994, 1995, 1996, 2000, 2001, 2002. Used by permission of NavPress Publishing Group.

Scripture quotations marked (NIV) are taken from the *Holy Bible, New International Version*®, NIV®. Copyright © 1973, 1978, 1984 by Biblica, Inc.™ Used by permission of Zondervan. All rights reserved worldwide. www.zondervan.com

Scripture quotations marked (NKJV) are taken from the New King James Version. Copyright © 1982 by Thmas Nelson, Inc. Used by permission. All rights reserved.

Scripture quotations marked (GNT) are from the *Good News Translation* in Today's English Version- Second Edition Copyright © 1992 by American Bible Society. Used by Permission.

Published in the United States by Credo House Publishers,
a division of Credo Communications LLC, Grand Rapids, Michigan
www.credohousepublishers.com

Cover design by Rtor Maghuyop
Interior design by Gram Telen

Printed in the United States of America

ISBN: 978-1-625860-83-5

Contents

Foreword 7
Introduction 11
Waiting 19
Knowing: An Essential Ingredient 25
Trust: An Essential Ingredient 33
Obedience: The Critical Ingredient 53
Biblical Waiters 63
Twenty-First Century Waiters 89
Consequences of Refusing to Wait on God 107
Benefits of Waiting on God 117
Afterword 125
Notes 129

Foreword

"But I want it now!"

As a parent, that is something I have heard countless times. It is the natural tendency of every child to be selfish and impatient. The problem that many adults have is that they have never grown out of those childish impulses. I remember when I finished my student teaching after four years of college and countless hours in a classroom. From the time I had been in third grade, I just knew I was going to be a teacher when I grew up. Things, however, didn't go as I had planned. My experience in that sixth grade class was awful (to put it mildly). In the end, I finished the semester, received a diploma and a certificate, but only barely. In fact, my college advisor gave me a pep talk with phrases like "It's a red flag to those who would hire you", and "It'll be difficult to find a position with this final evaluation." After fifteen years of hoping, preparing, dreaming, and spending tens of thousands of dollars, I had no motivation to pursue a teaching career. Worse yet, I had no idea what I was going to do next. So I spent the next six years trying to find my way.

It was a very difficult time.

I also remember the morning I got a phone call while I was at work. I had been waiting six weeks for the results of a biopsy. Over the phone my doctor told me "You have lymphoma, and I would recommend you see an oncologist right away." The weight of what that meant didn't sink in until I took a few minutes after the call and looked up what the words *lymphoma* and *oncologist* actually meant. Strangely, because of the good changes that had been happening in my life in the previous fifteen years since I finished college, primarily getting to know and trust God, the months that followed my cancer diagnosis were some of the best days of my life. I had no choice but to rely completely on God. As a result of this, my relationship with my wife went to a much deeper level, my priorities became much clearer, and I experienced how the body of Christ (the global Church) can rally behind a person in need. And that is just the beginning of it all.

Since I was given the "cancer free" news over four years ago, God has opened opportunities for me that I would have never realized apart from the journey through cancer. He has allowed me to be a source of encouragement, support, and advice for others who have had cancer impact their life.

It has been a wonderful time.

In both of these cases, following my student teaching and then dealing with cancer, I was in a circumstance that was outside of my control. I had to search for an answer. I had to put some things behind me, change my course, and move in a new direction. I had to wait.

After college, I did not wait well, and I struggled.

After my cancer diagnosis, I did wait well, and I am extremely grateful for what has resulted.

In the past three years, I have gotten to know Mary and have become familiar with some of the difficult circumstances that she has had to endure. I also know how hard it has been for her these past months to truly wait; however, I believe it has also been rewarding for her.

In her book, *When Doing Isn't Enough*, Mary articulates very clearly numerous biblical examples of those who have waited. In some cases, the biblical characters handled the opportunity well; and in other times, it turned out poorly. She balances the stories of biblical waiters with her own story as well as the stories of other twenty-first century waiters. She has the hope and belief that her own story and the stories of others who have waited will be beneficial to those who hear them.

I can't wait (pun intended) to see the wonderful things that will happen in her life as she faithfully waits for God's guidance. I am also excited to see how this book will help others. I hope that, through reading *When Doing Isn't Enough*, you will be inspired to trust God with whatever you are going through. I have seen in my own life, and in Mary's life, that God does great things in (and through) the lives of those who choose to wait for him and do things in his way on his time schedule.

Blessings!

—Rusty Miller
Celebrate Recovery Pennsylvania
State Representative

Introduction

Some lessons need to be learned, then relearned over and over again. Somehow, one learning experience is not quite enough for the more difficult or the more important lessons. For me, I had to be put in a Crock-Pot to learn two difficult and important lessons that I desperately needed to learn.

In 2003, I participated in a Bible study titled *Experiencing God* by Henry T. Blackaby and Claude V. King. The course contained twelve lessons. We covered one lesson per week. Out of all the reading and writing and discussion that took place over that twelve-week period, the only thing that stuck with me was the following phrase: "Don't just do something. Stand there."[1] As a task-oriented individual who has historically functioned as an overachiever, I had great difficulty wrapping my mind around this concept. Just being and not doing went against my grain on a very deep level.

In his book, *A Leader's Heart*, John Maxwell states, "God prepares leaders in a slow-cooker, not in a microwave oven."[2] Since I didn't learn the above lesson in 2003, God saw fit to put me in a Crock-Pot in 2004. I stayed in that slow-cooker for approximately two years. While I was simmering, God taught me that my source of self-esteem and self-worth is not in such external things as my achievements as I had always thought. He taught me that my worth has nothing to do with what I *do*, it has everything to do with *who* I am, i.e., a child of God. My worth derives from my relationship with him and I belong to him. I don't have to perform, achieve, take care of anyone, please others, or gain others approval in order for God to love me. He loves me no matter what, and he knew me and loved me before he placed me in my mother's womb. He also taught me to trust his plan and his timing on a much deeper level. He taught me to truly wait on him. "But those who wait on the Lord shall renew their strength; They shall mount up with wings like eagles, They shall run and not be weary, They shall walk and not faint" (Isaiah 40:31, NKJV).

Waiting on God means that you are willing to look to God for guidance and direction and are willing to abide by his timing regarding the events in your life. It means accepting that God knows better than you do what is in your best interest. It means putting God in the driver's seat of your life. Waiting on God requires surrendering to him.

"Waiting on Me means directing your attention to Me in hopeful anticipation of what I will do. It entails trusting Me with every fiber of your being instead of trying to figure things out yourself. Waiting on Me is the way I designed you to live: all day, every day. I created you to stay conscious of Me as you go about your daily duties."[3]

In light of all of this though, waiting on God is not passive waiting. It is not helpless waiting. It is not unproductive waiting. Waiting on God is active waiting. Waiting on God requires a conscious decision to trust God and wait on him no matter what, to not let fear run your life, and to live by faith, putting one foot in front of the other even when you can't see the path.

Waiting on God also requires a clear understanding of what I can do and what I cannot do, what I have control over and what I do not have control over. God will not do for us what we can do for ourselves. We need to do what we can do and leave to God the things we cannot do.

Over the course of the next nine years, I tried to weave these lessons into the fabric of my life. At times, I was successful, trusting God and waiting on him. At other times, I was not quite so successful, trusting myself and taking matters into my own hands.

When I allowed God to be in the driver's seat of my life, I experienced an internal peace and joy that surpasses all human understanding. The reason for this is because this peace and joy can only come from God. When I took matters into my own hands, I was looking for that peace and joy to come from human achievements and human relationships. What I received was the peace and joy that the world gives.

Having experienced both of these scenarios, I can tell you that the peace and joy that the world gives is hollow compared to the peace and joy that God gives. Nothing can compare to that deep certainty you feel when you know you are right where you are supposed to be, doing exactly what you were created to do. This peace and joy can *only* come from God. The Apostle John addressed this in one of his letters: "The world offers only a craving for physical pleasure, a craving for everything we see, and pride in our achievements and possessions. These are not from the Father, but are from this world" (1 John 2:16).

This is not to say that tolerating uncertainty and waiting on God is easy for me. It certainly is not. When I wait on God, fear often rears its ugly head. My natural inclination to take matters into my own hands also tends to rear its ugly head. At these times, I remind myself of some of God's promises to take care of me, such as:

- "If you'll hold on to me for dear life," says God, "I'll get you out of any trouble. I'll give you the best of care if you'll only get to know and trust me. Call me and I'll answer, be at your side in bad times; I'll rescue you, then throw you a party. I'll give you a long life, give you a long drink of salvation" (Psalm 91:14–16, MSG).

- "I'll take the hand of those who don't know the way, who can't see where they're going. I'll be a personal guide to them, directing them through unknown country. I'll be right there to

- "When you're in over your head, I'll be there with you. When you're in rough waters, you will not go down. When you're between a rock and a hard place, it won't be a dead end—Because I am God, your personal God, the Holy of Israel, your Savior" (Isaiah 43:2–3, MSG).

- "And don't be concerned about what to eat and what to drink. Don't worry about such things. These things dominate the thoughts of unbelievers all over the world, but your Father already knows your needs. Seek the Kingdom of God above all else, and he will give you everything you need" (Luke 12:29–31).

When I wait on God, I choose to trust him regardless of how I feel. The promise I hold on to the most is the promise Jesus made to His disciples immediately before he ascended into heaven. That promise is "I am with you always, even to the end of the age" (Matthew 28:20).

In September 2013, I attempted (once again) to incorporate these two lessons into my life. I stepped out of leadership of a ministry in which I had been serving. I also started attending a new church. When I began attending this new church, I made a conscious decision that I was not going to jump right in to service (the norm for me). I decided to wait on God. I told myself, God, and a few well-chosen individuals that the only way I would serve in ministry again would be if God asked me to. Then, in November, the senior pastor preached a message titled Paying It Forward, i.e., using our spiritual gifts, abilities, and passions to serve in the body of Christ. That message got me all fired up, and I asked to meet with one of the pastors to tell him what my spiritual gifts, abilities, and passions are and to discuss how I could best be utilized in this congregation. He suggested I serve in one of their ministries and introduced me to the director of that particular ministry. I told them I would think about it and pray about it and get back to them.

Over the next several days, I became increasingly uneasy, even agitated. I gradually came to the conclusion that serving in this ministry was not God's will for me. The words "Don't just do something. Stand there!" found their way out of the cobwebs in my mind and planted themselves firmly in the forefront of my consciousness. I realized that I had stopped waiting on God and, once again, took matters into my own hands. As soon as I became convinced that this was not the time and/or place for me to serve, I contacted both the pastor and the director of this particular ministry and told them both that I was not going to serve right now, that I was going back to waiting on God. Both were very gracious and understanding.

About the same time, I ran across the following card online: "Until God opens the next door, praise him in the hallway" (Crosscards.com). This resonated with me. My third book was in production and I did not have another one percolating inside me. I also was no longer leading a ministry. I was in a hallway and had run out of doors to open. As an action-oriented, doing kind of person, this was an uncomfortable place to be. I knew though, that God was going to have to provide the next opportunity for me and open the next door for me to walk through. I knew I would not be able to do it on my own. So in this time of uncertainty, I am waiting and trusting, praising him in the hallway.

Waiting

"If you want to work with Me, you have to accept My time frame. Hurry is not in my nature. Abraham and Sarah had to wait many years for the fulfillment of My promise, a son. How their long wait intensified their enjoyment of this child! *Faith is the assurance of things hoped for, perceiving as real fact what is not revealed to the senses.*"[1]

Waiting is not popular in our modern society. Immediate gratification is popular. We want what we want now, and we do everything possible to get whatever it is we want now and avoid waiting. Sometimes, waiting is unavoidable though and we have no choice but to wait.

We have all experienced times of waiting in our lives. We might not have liked it or chosen it; however, we have experienced it. We may have tolerated it or hated it or waited in anger or waited in fear or waited in expectancy. We may have decided to put the time to good use like reading a book or working on a laptop while in a waiting room or we may have paced or we may have slept. We may have smoked cigarettes or drank coffee or did any combination of any of these or any other of a multitude of additional coping mechanisms. However we have chosen to wait though, we have waited.

Merriam-Webster Dictionary defines *wait* as "to stay in a place until an expected event happens, until someone arrives, until it is your turn to do something, etc.; to not do something until something else happens; to remain in a state in which you expect or hope that something will happen soon."

God appears to like waiting and seems to require it of anyone who will be used by him, particularly those who will be used in a significant way. When studying the lives of individuals in the Bible who have been used by God to accomplish extraordinary tasks, there certainly seems to be a correlation between waiting and serving God in the extraordinary ways they were called to serve. Even Jesus had an extended period of waiting before he was able to engage in the work he had come to earth to do. Luke 3:23 tells us, "Jesus was about thirty years old when he began his public ministry."

Jesus Waited

Much is written about Jesus's birth and infancy. The birth of Jesus is recorded in Luke 2:1–7 and in Matthew 1:18–21 and 24–25. Luke 2:8–20 tells of the shepherds in the fields near Bethlehem visiting the newborn Jesus. Luke 2:21–38 tells of eight-day old Jesus being circumcised and taken to the Temple in Jerusalem so Mary and Joseph could perform the ritual required by the law of Moses when a child is born. Matthew 2:1–12 tells of the wise men's visit to the baby Jesus. Matthew 2:13–15 tells of the journey Mary, Joseph, and the baby Jesus took from Bethlehem to Egypt. Matthew 2:19–23 then tells of the family leaving Egypt and settling in Nazareth.

Following those accounts, all that is then written about Jesus's childhood is "There the child grew up healthy and strong. He was filled with wisdom, and God's favor was on him" (Luke 2:40).

The next scriptural account of Jesus's life describes an incident that occurred when he was twelve years old.

> Every year Jesus' parents traveled to Jerusalem for the Feast of Passover. When he was twelve years old, they went up as they always did for the Feast. When it was over and they left for home, the child Jesus stayed behind in Jerusalem, but his parents didn't know it. Thinking he was somewhere in the company of pilgrims, they journeyed for a whole day and then began looking for him among relatives and neighbors. When they didn't find him, they went back to Jerusalem looking for him. The next day they found him in the Temple seated among the teachers, listening to them and asking questions. The teachers were all quite taken with him, impressed with the sharpness of his answers. But his parents were not impressed; they were upset and hurt. His mother said, "Young man, why have you done this to us? Your father and

> I have been half out of our minds looking for you." He said, "Why were you looking for me? Didn't you know that I had to be here, dealing with the things of my Father?"
>
> Luke 2:41–49 (MSG)

Following this exchange, "He returned to Nazareth with them and was obedient to them" (Luke 2:51). The only scriptural account of his growing up years following this incident is "Jesus grew in wisdom and in stature and in favor with God and all the people" (Luke 2:52).

He waited from the time he was twelve until the time he was thirty to deal with the things of his Father. That is a lot of years of waiting, and we can only speculate what those years might have been like for Jesus. I imagine that he might have had very mixed emotions about beginning the work he had come to earth to do, i.e., an eager anticipation to begin the teaching, preaching, and healing aspect of his ministry as well as dread about the culmination of his earthly ministry, his crucifixion. I am also imagining that those years were a time of preparation for him and that he waited out of obedience to his Father, beginning his public ministry when his Father let him know the time was right.

With the exception of Jesus, each of the individuals who will be discussed in this book is an ordinary human being. They are not superheroes or extraordinary people. They are ordinary human beings called to do extraordinary things and prepared by God to accomplish these things. Part of that preparation was a time of waiting.

In order to be willing to wait on God and to wait on him effectively, one must know him, trust him, and be willing to obey him.

Knowing: An Essential Ingredient

If one is to willingly agree to wait on God, one first has to know God, the *real* God, not a distorted image of God. The real God is love. He doesn't have love. He doesn't show love. He *is* love. It's his character. The Apostle John explained this in one of the letters he wrote to the early church. "God is love, and all who live in love live in God, and God lives in them" (1 John 4:16).

Centuries before, King David spoke about God's character in Psalm 103.

> The Lord is compassionate and merciful, slow to get angry and filled with unfailing love.... For his unfailing love toward those who fear him is as great as the height of the heavens above the earth.... The Lord is like a father to his children, tender and compassionate to those who fear him.
>
> Psalm 103:8, 11, 13

Fearing God

Before we go any further, the concept of fearing God needs to be addressed. Biblical fear of God is not the same as being afraid that we'll be hurt or scared of a harsh punishment. It is more like awe or respect. God himself spoke of this kind of fear through the prophet Jeremiah. "Have you no respect for me? Why don't you tremble in my presence?" (Jeremiah 5:22). The writer of the Book of Acts also spoke of this kind of fear when he said: "The story of what happened spread quickly all through Ephesus, to Jews and Greeks alike. A solemn fear descended on the city, and the name of the Lord Jesus was greatly honored" (Acts 19:17). So if one fears God with a biblical fear, one is in awe of God. One respects and honors him. If one fears God with a worldly fear, one is afraid that God will mete out harsh punishment and/or withdraw his love.

Growing up, I learned to see God as anything but loving. I learned that his love was conditional and that I had to earn his love through performing good works. I also learned to see him as a punishing God who was distant, critical, and judgmental and who didn't care about how I felt or what I needed. I was afraid of him with a worldly fear, not a biblical fear.

The process I went through to get to know the real God involved immersing myself in an extensive period of questioning, studying, and deciding what I believed and what I didn't believe. The result of this was that I finally began to understand that the real God was not the God I had learned about in my childhood. I began to believe that God really does love me and care about how I feel. I was realizing that God knows what I need and that he will take care of me and provide for me. I spent months reading Matthew 6:25–33 every day, and I slowly began to believe that if God takes care of the birds and the flowers, he will take care of me. I began to see God as my heavenly parent who loves me with a perfect love. Matthew 6:25–33 is as follows:

> That is why I tell you not to worry about everyday life—whether you have enough food and drink, or enough clothes to wear. Isn't life more than food, and your body more than clothing? Look at the birds. They don't plant or harvest or store food in barns for your heavenly Father feeds them. And aren't you more valuable to him than they are? Can all your worries add a single moment to your life? And why worry about your clothing? Look at the lilies of the field and how they grow. They don't work or make their clothing, yet Solomon in all his glory was not dressed as beautifully as they are. And if God cares so wonderfully for wildflowers that are here today and thrown into the fire tomorrow, he will certainly care for you. Why do you have so little faith? So don't worry about these things, saying, 'What will we eat? What will we drink? What will we wear?' These things dominate the thoughts of unbelievers, but your heavenly Father already knows all your needs. Seek the Kingdom of God above all else, and live righteously, and he will give you everything you need.

Important Note: Everything that God does for us he does out of love.

Though he loves us with a perfect love, he does not always give us everything we want or let us get away with bad behavior. Like any good parent, he gives his children what they need, *not* what they want. Sometimes he says no to us, sometimes he lets us experience the consequences of our choices and actions, and sometimes he disciplines us when we disobey him. He doesn't discipline us because he's angry at us or disappointed in us. He disciplines us because he loves us.

The Apostle Paul spoke about the power of God's love in his letter to the church in Rome.

> And I am convinced that nothing can ever separate us from God's love. Neither death nor life, neither angels nor demons, neither our fears for today nor our worries about tomorrow—not even the powers of hell can separate us from God's love.
>
> No power in the sky above or in the earth below—indeed, nothing in all creation will ever be able to separate us from the love of God that is revealed in Christ Jesus our Lord.
>
> Romans 8:38–39

He spoke about the breadth of God's love in his letter to the church in Ephesus: "And may you have the power to understand, as all God's people should, how wide, how long, how high, and how deep his love is. May you experience the love of Christ, though it is too great to understand fully" (Ephesians 3:18-19).

God in the Flesh

If you have a hard time thinking of God as loving, think about Jesus. After all, Jesus was God with flesh on. Five days before his death, Jesus said the following words to a crowd in Jerusalem: "If you trust me, you are trusting not only me, but also God who sent me. For when you see me, you are seeing the one who sent me" (John 12:44–45).

Then think about what Jesus did for us. He left the glory of heaven to take on human form and do something for us which we were not able to do for ourselves. He created the way for us to get to heaven. He explained this to his disciple Nathaneal in the first chapter of the gospel of John, verse 51: "Then he said, 'I tell you the truth, you will all see heaven open and the angels of God going up and down on the Son of Man, the one who is the stairway between heaven and earth.'"

Jesus understood that the reason he had come to earth was to offer himself as a sacrifice for the sins and wrongdoings of all mankind. Throughout the three years of his earthly ministry, he never lost sight of his purpose: "The Son of Man must be lifted up, so that everyone who believes in him will have eternal life" (John 3:14–15). As Jesus went about ministering to people by teaching them and healing them, he was always moving toward the fulfillment of his purpose. "Jesus went through the towns and villages, teaching as he went, always pressing on toward Jerusalem" (Luke 13:22).

If you want a picture of pure, perfect love, picture Jesus bloody and beaten beyond recognition hanging on a wooden cross. He did not have to stay hanging there. He *chose* to stay hanging there. It was not nails that held him to that cross. It was love, love for each and every one of us, past, present, and future.

Love is not a feeling. It is an action. It is a choice. We can choose to *act* loving, even when we don't *feel* loving. Jesus chose to act loving by carrying his cross to Calvary in Jerusalem and allowing Roman soldiers to nail him to it, then staying nailed to it until he died. We get a glimpse of how Jesus felt about going to the cross in the account of him praying in the Garden of Gethsemane prior to his arrest.

> He walked away, about a stone's throw, and knelt down and prayed, "Father, if you are willing, please take this cup of suffering away from me. Yet I want your will to be done, not mine." Then an angel from heaven appeared and strengthened him. He prayed more fervently, and he was in such agony of spirit that his sweat fell to the ground like great drops of blood.
>
> Luke 22:41–44

It is important to note that Jesus went to the cross out of obedience to his father and love for us. It was a choice he made *in spite of* how he was feeling. Prior to his arrest, Jesus spoke to the apostles about the choice he was making. He said, "No one can take my life from me. I sacrifice it voluntarily. For I have the authority to lay it down when I want to and also to take it up again.

For this is what my Father has commanded" (John 10:18). He also stated, "There is no greater love than to lay down one's life for one's friends" (John 15:13).

John spoke about this expression of God's love. "God showed how much he loved us by sending his one and only Son into the world so that we might have eternal life through him. This is real love—not that we loved God, but that he loved us and sent his Son as a sacrifice to take away our sins" (1 John 4:9-10).

In the *Experiencing God* curriculum, Blackaby states, "In the death and resurrection of Jesus Christ, God forever convinced me that he loved me. The cross, the death of Jesus Christ, and His resurrection are God's final, total, and complete expression that He loves us."[1]

This convinced me too. Once I understood and accepted and *knew* that God loved me and that the ultimate expression of his love is Jesus bloody and beaten beyond recognition hanging on a cross, I couldn't help but love him back. It was my natural reaction and I put him in the driver's seat of my life. I then began to live my life for an audience of One. Human approval, once the most important thing to me, was no longer so important.

Trust: An Essential Ingredient

Trust is inherent in waiting. Merriam-Webster Dictionary defines *trust* as "belief that someone or something is reliable, good, honest, effective; assured reliance on the character, ability, strength, or truth of someone or something; dependence on something future or contingent: hope." It's easy to trust God when everything is going well for us, when our life circumstances and situations are in our favor. It's not so easy to trust him when life seems to turn against us.

Two biblical characters who manifested extraordinary trust in God in spite of horrendous life circumstances were Joseph and Job. Among biblical scholars it is commonly believed that they lived at approximately the same time in history, 2200–1800 BC.

Joseph's story

After Adam and Eve left the Garden of Eden, the human race grew and multiplied and became very evil.

The only individual that did not do evil in God's sight was Noah. Due to this, God told Noah that he planned to destroy the evil human race with a great flood. God also told Noah that he intended to save Noah and his family from the flood, and as always, God made good on his word and did indeed save Noah and his family from the flood.

Following the flood, the human race once again grew and multiplied. God then created a people who were set apart to belong to him, to be his family. God chose Abraham to be the father of his family. Abraham and his wife, Sarah, gave birth to Isaac. Isaac and his wife, Rebekah, gave birth to two sons, one of whom was Jacob. Jacob (later renamed Israel by God) had twelve sons and numerous daughters by various wives. One of those sons was Joseph.

> Jacob loved Joseph more than any of his other children because Joseph had been born to him in his old age. So one day Jacob had a special gift made for Joseph—a beautiful robe. But his brothers hated Joseph because their father loved him more than the rest of them. They couldn't say a kind word to him.
>
> Genesis 37:3–4

The brothers' hatred and jealousy of Joseph was fueled even more when Joseph told them of two dreams he had in which the imagery of the dream seemed to convey that he would one day rule over them. This hatred and jealousy eventually culminated in the brothers selling Joseph to some Ishmaelites, who were Midianite traders. The traders took Joseph to Egypt, and his brothers deceived their father into thinking that Joseph was dead by dipping the robe Jacob had made for Joseph into goat's blood and telling Jacob they had found the blood-stained robe. "Then Jacob tore his clothes and dressed himself in burlap. He mourned deeply for his son for a long time" (Genesis 37:34). "Meanwhile, the Midianite traders arrived in Egypt, where they sold Joseph to Potiphar, an officer of Pharaoh, the king of Egypt. Potiphar was captain of the palace guard" (Genesis 37:36).

God did not abandon Joseph when he was sold into slavery in Egypt. On the contrary, God had his eye on Joseph and protected him, showering him with special blessings.

> The Lord was with Joseph so he succeeded in everything he did as he served in the home of his Egyptian master. Potiphar noticed this and realized that the Lord was with Joseph, giving him success in everything he did. This pleased Potiphar so he soon made Joseph his personal attendant. He put him in charge of his entire household and everything he owned.
>
> Genesis 39:2-4

Potiphar's wife was sexually attracted to Joseph and tried to seduce him on numerous occasions. Joseph refused all of her advances. One day, she grabbed him by his cloak. He pulled away from her and fled, leaving his cloak in her hands. She told her servants and her husband that Joseph had tried to rape her and showed them his cloak as proof. "Potiphar was furious when he heard his wife's story about how Joseph had treated her. So he took Joseph and threw him into the prison where the king's prisoners were held, and there he remained" (Genesis 39:19–20).

God continued to watch over Joseph while he was in prison and Joseph continued to trust in God's care of him. "And the Lord made Joseph a favorite with the prison warden. Before long, the warden put Joseph in charge of all the other prisoners and over everything that happened in the prison" (Genesis 39:21–22). While in prison, Joseph interpreted the dreams of two other prisoners. Both of these prisoners had been servants of the king. The dream interpretations involved predictions of what was going to happen to these two men. Both of the predictions came true. A few years later, Pharaoh had two dreams that disturbed him and that none of his wise men could interpret. One of the prisoners whose dream Joseph had correctly interpreted and who was now back in the king's service told Pharaoh of his experience with Joseph.

> Pharaoh sent for Joseph at once, and he was quickly brought from the prison. Pharaoh said to Joseph, "I had a dream last night, and no one here can tell me what it means. But I have heard that when you hear about a dream you can interpret it." "It is beyond my power to do this," Joseph replied, "But God can tell you what it means and set you at ease."
>
> Genesis 41:14–16

Joseph then interpreted Pharaoh's dreams to him, telling Pharaoh that Egypt would experience seven years of plenty followed by seven years of famine. Pharaoh believed and trusted the interpretations Joseph gave him.

> Then Pharaoh said to Joseph, "Since God has revealed the meaning of the dreams to you, clearly no one else is as intelligent or wise as you are. You will be in charge of my court, and all my people will take orders from you. Only I, sitting on my throne, will have a rank higher than yours." Pharaoh said to Joseph, "I hereby put you in charge of the entire land of Egypt. I am Pharaoh, but no one will lift a hand or foot in the entire land of Egypt without your approval."
>
> Genesis 41:39–41, 44

Important Note: Joseph did not trust in his own ability to interpret the dreams. He trusted in God's ability to do this through him, and he gave all the credit and the glory to God.

During the seven years of plenty, Joseph oversaw the storing of grain from the Egyptian crops in huge storehouses. When the famine hit, the grain was distributed to the people of Egypt according to Joseph's instructions. The famine also impacted the nations surrounding Egypt, including the land of Canaan where Jacob and his family lived. Jacob sent ten of his sons to Egypt to buy grain. "Since Joseph was governor of all Egypt and in charge of selling grain to all the people, it was to him that his brothers came.... Although Joseph recognized his brothers, they did not recognize him" (Genesis 42:6, 8). Joseph did not reveal his identity to his brothers. Instead, he gave them grain and supplies for their journey home. He also told them to bring their other brother to him and put one of the ten brothers in prison as a ransom. When the brothers returned with the eleventh brother, Joseph finally revealed his identity to them.

> Joseph could stand it no longer. There were many people in the room, and he said to his attendants, "Out, all of you!" So he was alone with his brothers when he told them who he was. Then he broke down and wept.
> He wept so loudly the Egyptians could hear him, and word of it quickly carried to Pharaoh's palace. "I am Joseph!" he said to his brothers. "Is my father still alive?" But his brothers were speechless! They were stunned to realize that Joseph was standing there in front of them.
>
> Genesis 45:1–3

> "But don't be upset, and don't be angry with yourselves for selling me to this place. It was God who sent me here ahead of you to preserve your lives. This famine that has ravaged the land for two years will last five more years, and there will be neither plowing nor harvesting. God has sent me ahead of you to keep you and your families alive and to preserve many survivors. So it was God who sent me here, not you! And he is the one who made me an adviser to

Pharaoh—the manager of his entire palace and the governor of all Egypt."

Genesis 45:5–8

Note: Joseph again gave all the credit and glory to God. He did not attribute his achievements to his own abilities. He attributed them to God's plan and he trusted in God's plan.

Joseph and his brothers had a long tearful reunion. As Pharaoh had been made aware of the arrival of Joseph's brothers, Pharaoh instructed Joseph to have his father and brothers and all of their families relocate to Egypt so Joseph could ensure that they were fed during the remaining five years of famine. "So Jacob and his entire family went to Egypt—sons and grandsons, daughters and granddaughters—all his descendants" (Genesis 46:6–7). Joseph took care of his family, providing for them during the years of the famine and beyond. "Joseph lived to the age of 110. 'Soon I will die,' Joseph told his brothers, 'but God will surely come to help you and lead you out of this land of Egypt. He will bring you back to the land he solemnly promised to give to Abraham, to Isaac, and to Jacob'" (Genesis 50:22, 24).

This is how it happened that the nation of Israel, the Hebrews, settled in Egypt.

There is no indication in scripture that Joseph ever lost faith in God or stopped trusting him. Joseph continued to live his life in a Godly way in whatever circumstance he found himself. Job did the same.

Job's Story

> There once was a man named Job who lived in the land of Uz. He was blameless—a man of complete integrity. He feared God and stayed away from evil.... He was, in fact, the richest person in that entire area.
>
> Job 1:1, 3

Job's life then radically changed. Job 1:6–12 makes it clear that what was about to happen to Job was an expression of spiritual warfare.

> One day the members of the heavenly court came to present themselves before the Lord, and the Accuser, Satan, came with them. "Where have you come from?" the Lord asked Satan. Satan answered the Lord, "I have been patrolling the earth, watching everything that's going on." Then the Lord asked Satan, "Have you noticed my servant Job? He is the finest man in all the earth. He is blameless—a man of complete integrity. He fears God and stays away from evil." Satan replied to the Lord, "Yes, but Job has good reason to fear God. You have always put a wall of protection around him and his home and his property. You have made him prosper in everything he does. Look how rich he is! But reach out and take away everything he has, and he will surely curse you to your face!" "All right, you may test him," the Lord said to Satan. "Do whatever you want with everything

he possesses, but don't harm him physically." So Satan left the Lord's presence.

Job 1:6–12

Note about Spiritual Warfare

I imagine many of you have conflicting thoughts and feelings about spiritual warfare and are not even sure it exists. Take heart, you are not alone. For many years, I did not believe that spiritual warfare was real. I thought that people who talked about spiritual warfare were wacky. That was until I started experiencing it myself. I then started to research it and found that three New Testament writers discussed it in the Bible.

The Apostle Paul told the church in Ephesus: "For we are not fighting against flesh-and-blood enemies, but against evil rulers and authorities of the unseen world, against mighty powers in this dark world, and against evil spirits in the heavenly places" (Ephesians 6:12).

The Apostle Peter told Jewish Christians: "Stay alert! Watch out for your great enemy, the devil. He prowls around like a roaring lion, looking for someone to devour" (1 Peter 5:8).

Finally, the Apostle John explained how Satan came into being: "Then there was war in heaven. Michael and his angels fought against the dragon and his angels. And the dragon lost the battle, and he and his angels were forced out of heaven. This great dragon—the ancient serpent called the devil, or Satan, the one deceiving the whole world—was thrown down to the earth with all his angels...And the dragon was angry at the woman and declared war against the rest of her children—all who keep God's commandments and maintain their testimony for Jesus" (Revelation 12:7–9, 17).

So Satan and his angels are alive and well, roaming the earth with the sole purpose of sabotaging anyone who is committed to Christ and furthering God's kingdom on earth.

Back to Job

After Satan left the Lord's presence, he arranged for Job's oxen and donkeys to be stolen and his farmhands to be killed, his sheep and shepherds to be killed, camels to be stolen, servants to be killed, and finally, all his children to be killed. Job's reaction to this was: "Job stood up and tore his robe in grief. Then he shaved his head and fell to the ground to worship. He said, 'I came naked from my mother's womb, and I will be naked when I leave. The Lord gave me what I had, and the Lord has taken it away. Praise the name of the Lord!' In all of this, Job did not sin by blaming God" (Job 1:20–22).

Satan then went before God again and asked permission to take away Job's health.

> "All right, do with him as you please," the Lord said to Satan. "But spare his life." So Satan left the Lord's presence, and he struck Job with terrible boils from head to foot. Job scraped his skin with a piece of broken pottery as he sat among the ashes. His wife said to him, "Are

you still trying to maintain your integrity? Curse God and die." But Job replied, "You talk like a foolish woman. Should we accept only good things from the hand of God and never anything bad?" So in all this, Job said nothing wrong.

Job 2:6–10

Three friends of Job (Eliphaz, Bildad and Zophar) then came to visit him as they had each learned of what he was going through. "When they saw Job from a distance, they scarcely recognized him. Wailing loudly, they tore their robes and threw dust into the air over their heads to show their grief. Then they sat on the ground with him for seven days and nights. No one said a word to Job, for they saw that his suffering was too great for words. At last Job spoke…" (Job 2:12–13, 3:1).

When Job finally spoke, he expressed his anguish in an authentic and raw way. "I wish I had died in my mother's womb or died the moment I was born… Instead of eating I mourn, and I can never stop groaning. Everything I fear and dread comes true. I have no peace, no rest, and my troubles never end" (Job 3:11, 24–26, GNT). Each of Job's friends responded to him individually; however, each communicated the same message to him, that is, he was to blame for what was happening to him. Eliphaz told him, "Evil does not grow in the soil, nor does trouble grow out of the ground. No! Man brings trouble on himself, as surely as sparks fly up from a fire" (Job 5:6–7, GNT). Bildad said, "Your children must have sinned against God, and so he punished them as they deserved" (Job 8:4, GNT). Zophar's contribution was "God is punishing you less than you deserve... God knows which men are worthless; he sees all their evil deeds...Put your heart right, Job. Reach out to God. Put away evil and wrong from your home" (Job 11:6, 11, 13–14, GNT).

When Job responded to his friends, he declared his innocence while maintaining his trust in God.

> You think you are better than I am, and regard my troubles as proof of my guilt. Can't you see it is God who has done this?... You are my friends! Take pity on me! The hand of God has struck me down. Why must you persecute me the way God does? Haven't you tormented me enough?... But I know there is someone in heaven who will come at last to my defense. Even after my skin is eaten by disease, while still in this body I will see God. I will see him with my own eyes, and he will not be a stranger.
>
> Job 19:5–6, 21–22, 25–27 (GNT)

> I follow faithfully the road he chooses, and never wander to either side. I always do what God commands; I follow his will, not my own desires...I tremble with fear before him.
>
> Job 23:11–12, 15 (GNT)

At one point, Job said, "I am torn apart by worry and pain; I have had day after day of suffering...I swear I have never acted wickedly and never tried to deceive others. Let God weigh me on honest scales, and he will see how innocent I am" (Job 30:27, 31:5–6, GNT).

At another point, God spoke to Job directly, saying:

> Who are you to question my wisdom with your ignorant, empty words? Stand up now like a man and answer the questions I ask you. Were you there when I made the world? If you know so much, tell me about it. Who decided how large it would be? Who stretched the measuring line over it? Do you know all the answers? What holds up the pillars that support the earth? Who laid the cornerstone of the world?... Job, you challenged Almighty God: will you give up now, or will you answer?
>
> Job 38:2–6, 40:2 (GNT)

Job answered him, "I spoke foolishly, Lord. What can I answer? I will not try to say anything else. I have already said more than I should" (Job 40:4–5, GNT). The Lord spoke to Job again, saying, "Stand up now like a man, and answer my questions. Are you trying to prove that I am unjust—to put me in the wrong and yourself in the right? Are you as strong as I am? Can your voice thunder as loud as mine? If so, stand up in your honor and pride; clothe yourself with majesty and glory" (Job 40:7–10, GNT).

Job responded to this with repentance and the Lord blessed him beyond his wildest dreams. Job's response:

> I know, Lord, that you are all-powerful; that you can do everything you want. You ask how I dare question your wisdom when I am so very ignorant. I talked about things I did not understand, about marvels too great for me to

know. You told me to listen while you spoke and to try to answer your questions. In the past I knew only what others had told me, but now I have seen you with my own eyes. So I am ashamed of all I have said and repent in dust and ashes.

Job 42:2–6 (GNT)

The Lord restored his fortunes. In fact, the Lord gave him twice as much as before!... So the Lord blessed Job in the second half of his life even more than in the beginning...Job lived 140 years after that, living to see four generations of his children and grandchildren. Then he died, an old man who had lived a long, full life.

Job 42:10, 12, 16–17

Job was blessed greatly by God for maintaining faith and trust in him when unbelievable tragedy enveloped his life. I wonder how many of us today would stay loyal to God, maintaining trust in him, while experiencing such tragedy. I know one person who did. Her name is Amy. She trusted in the Great Physician when diagnosed with cancer, and God blessed her greatly for that trust.

Amy's Story

Pregnant with her first child, Amy was feeling much joyful anticipation. This baby was wanted, hoped for, and planned. Then, seventeen weeks into her pregnancy in December 2002, her life as she knew it came to an abrupt halt. She was diagnosed with acute lymphocytic leukemia and told she would probably lose the baby. A port was implanted for chemotherapy, an ultrasound was done to get a baseline on the baby's growth, and treatment began. In recalling this time, Amy stated, "Everyone around me was freaking out. I felt this strange peace, this strange comfort. God was telling me that everything was going to be okay. I felt like my baby was wrapped in a protective bubble."

Where did this peace and comfort come from? It came from a lifetime of seeing faith and trust modeled in front of her eyes. Her parents were very active members of a Southern Baptist congregation who not only talked the talk, they walked the walk. Throughout her childhood, her parents consistently trusted God when they fell on hard times and thanked him when they experienced bounty. Amy stated that she would always hear her parents say, "God will provide" during times of scarcity and "Thank you Lord for the blessing" during times of plenty. As a result of this, the seeds of faith were planted in Amy at a very early age.

Jesus talked about seeds of faith in the gospel of Matthew.

> A farmer went out to plant some seeds. As he scattered them across his field, some seeds fell on a footpath, and the birds came out and ate them. Other seeds fell on shallow soil with underlying rock. The seeds sprouted quickly because the soil was shallow. But the plants soon wilted under the hot sun, and since they didn't have deep roots, they died. Other seeds

fell among thorns that grew up and choked out the tender plants.

Still other seeds fell on fertile soil, and they produced a crop that was thirty, sixty, and even a hundred times as much as had been planted!

Now listen to the explanation of the parable about the farmer planting seeds: The seed that fell on the footpath represents those who hear the message about the Kingdom and don't understand it. Then the evil one comes and snatches away the seed that was planted in their hearts. The seed on the rocky soil represents those who hear the message and immediately receive it with joy.

But since they don't have deep roots, they don't last long. They fall away as soon as they have problems or are persecuted for believing God's word. The seed that fell among the thorns represents those who hear God's word, but all too quickly the message is crowded out by the worries of this life and the lure of wealth, so no fruit is produced. The seed that fell on good soil represents those who truly hear and understand God's word and produce a harvest of thirty, sixty, or even a hundred times as much as had been planted!

Matthew 13:3–8, 18–23

Amy obviously provided good soil for the seeds to be planted in. She came to a personal saving faith in Christ in her early teens. She knew that God would provide for her and she trusted him in her head. That faith and trust moved to her heart when she was diagnosed with cancer and "had to really call on God and trust him." The words she had been hearing and saying all her life took on much deeper meaning as she "lived it." The seeds of faith that had been planted in her childhood "took root" and planted themselves firmly and permanently in her heart. Like her parents, she began to truly walk the walk, not just talk the talk. She describes this period of her life as "a time of spiritual maturity."

Another contributing factor to the peace she experienced during this time was that she had been placed on many prayer chains. Knowing that people all over the globe were "lifting me up" added to the peace and comfort she was experiencing.

God rewarded Amy's faith and trust in him with multiple miracles. The first miracle was that immediately after her diagnosis, her doctor was able to get her admitted to Wake Forest University Hospital in North Carolina, the number 3 hospital in the country for the treatment of leukemia. The next miracle was that though she was a few hours away from the nearest friend or family member, she was never alone while there. She was discharged after three weeks even though she had been told that she would be there four to six weeks—miracle number 3. Her care was then transferred to Hershey Medical Center in Hershey, Pennsylvania, close to her home.

While at Hershey, she received countless dosages of chemotherapy, twelve shots of chemotherapy into her spinal column, and approximately fifty blood and platelet transfusions. Throughout this whole process, she felt a very close bond with her unborn baby. She knew she was not alone. She knew that she and her child were going through this together.

As the plan was to induce labor when Amy was thirty-four weeks pregnant, the cancer treatment was stopped one month before this to allow her blood counts to increase, thereby increasing the chances of a safe delivery. The plan worked. In April 2003, Amy gave birth to a four-pound, ten-ounce plump, pink baby girl. The baby's Apgar score was perfect. She was healthy and happy.

One week after the birth of her daughter, Amy was fitted with a mask for cranial radiation. She received ten to twelve low dose treatments of radiation to prevent recurrence in her brain or spinal column. She was then placed on a maintenance treatment of oral chemotherapy that continued for the next two years. Her blood count and immune system started to rebound and her hair started to grow back.

Throughout this process, Amy knew that she was in good medical hands. Though she trusted her doctors, her real faith and trust was in the Great Physician. She consistently asked God to give the medical professionals wisdom and to work through them. He did, and God rewarded her richly for placing her faith and trust in him.

When Amy was discharged from Wake Forest Hospital, she was considered to be in remission. Five years later, she was considered to be cured. In April 2007, as she was coming up on five years in remission, Amy and her husband decided to try to have a second child even though doctors at both Wake Forest and Hershey had told them it was unlikely Amy would be able to get pregnant again. In July 2007, they found out they were pregnant and in August found out that her womb held "three round perfect sacks." Amy and her husband were "in shock, overwhelmed, and nervous." Their focus shifted from worrying about the recurrence of the leukemia to the health of the triplets. Doctors were cautiously optimistic that all three babies would survive. Amy once again "called on God," and he, once again, came through for her. All three babies not only survived, they thrived. In February 2008, Amy gave birth to a four-pound, two-ounce son; a three-pound, eight-ounce daughter; and another daughter who weighed three pounds, five ounces. Each one was healthy, experiencing nothing uncommon to babies who are born prematurely. They were referred to as "feeders and growers" in the neonatal intensive care unit where they spent three weeks.

At the time of this writing, Amy is cancer-free and all four of her children are happy, healthy, and growing in God. Amy knows in the deepest part of her being that God healed her of cancer and gave her four healthy children. "Jesus looked at them intently and said, 'Humanly speaking, it is impossible. But with God everything is possible'" (Matthew 19:26).

Word of Caution

Though I truly believe that Amy's story is one of miraculous divine healing, I am not trying to convey here that God heals everyone who asks him to take away a physical or medical condition. I realize that healing doesn't always happen. Sometimes, people get injured or get sick and healing doesn't occur and they die or live broken lives or God does not provide the type of healing that is asked for. God may choose to provide emotional and/or spiritual healing, which enables the individual to cope with the medical condition.

I want to remind you of the Merriam-Webster definition of *trust*, i.e., "belief that someone or something is reliable, good, honest, effective; assured reliance on the character, ability, strength, or truth of someone or something; dependence on something future or contingent : hope." If we truly trust God, then we believe right down to our toes that he knows what is best for us and we abide by his will in all circumstances, up to and including death.

Obedience: The Critical Ingredient

When the Israelites left Egypt under Moses's leadership, "The Lord went ahead of them. He guided them during the day with a pillar of cloud, and he provided light at night with a pillar of fire. This allowed them to travel by day or by night. And the Lord did not remove the pillar of cloud or pillar of fire from its place in front of the people" (Exodus 13:21–22).

> This was the regular pattern—at night the cloud that covered the Tabernacle had the appearance of fire. Whenever the cloud lifted from over the sacred tent, the people of Israel would break camp and follow it. And wherever the cloud settled, the people of Israel would set up camp. In this way, they traveled and camped at the Lord's command wherever he told them to go. Then they remained in their camp as long as the cloud stayed over the Tabernacle. If the cloud remained over the Tabernacle for a long time, the Israelites stayed and performed their

duty to the Lord. Sometimes the cloud would stay over the Tabernacle for only a few days, so the people would stay for only a few days, as the Lord commanded. Then at the Lord's command they would break camp and move on. Sometimes the cloud stayed only overnight and lifted the next morning. But day or night, when the cloud lifted, the people broke camp and moved on. Whether the cloud stayed above the Tabernacle for two days, a month, or a year, the people of Israel stayed in camp and did not move on. But as soon as it lifted, they broke camp and moved on. So they camped or traveled at the Lord's command, and they did whatever the Lord told them through Moses.

Numbers 9:16–23

Whenever I read the account of how God guided the Israelites with the pillar of cloud and pillar of fire after they left Egypt, I am struck by how the people waited on God and obeyed him. As stated in the introduction, waiting on God means that you are willing to look to God for guidance and direction and that you are willing to abide by his timing regarding the events in your life, i.e., you are willing to obey him.

When the cloud lifted, the Israelites moved. When the cloud settled, they camped in the spot the cloud had settled in until the cloud lifted again. They didn't argue or try to move prematurely or try to set up camp somewhere else. They just followed the guidance of the Lord. They obeyed him. This made God smile and he released his blessings, his provisions, on them. He took care of them. He made sure the Israelites had quail and bread and water so they wouldn't die of thirst or starvation.

Another biblical example of obedience, an extraordinary and classic example in my opinion, is Noah. As stated in the third chapter, God told Noah that he planned to destroy the evil human race with a great flood. God also told Noah that he intended to save Noah and his family from the flood. In order for Noah and his family to survive the flood, God told Noah to build a boat, and when God told Noah to build this boat, Noah was in the middle of a desert! Can you imagine how ridiculous it must have seemed to the people around Noah that he was building a boat? Can you also imagine how much grief Noah and his family probably took because he was building a boat? Yet Noah did not let anything deter him. He did what God told him to do because he loved God and trusted him.

God wants this same kind of obedience from us. He wants us to obey him without question even when it seems to make no sense at all, *especially* when it makes no sense at all. Further, he wants us to obey him because we know him, trust him, love him, and fear him with biblical fear. He does not want us to fear him with a worldly fear. When we obey him out of love and biblical fear the result is twofold—God accomplishes his work in the world and our obedience deepens our relationship with him. Blackaby and King address this in *Experiencing God*.

> After God has taken the initiative to involve you in His work, you believe Him and adjust your

life to Him. Only then do you get to the place of obedience. You must obey Him first. Then, He will accomplish His work through you. When God does a God-sized work through your life, you come to know Him intimately by experience.[1]

This certainly has proven to be true for me. Fairly early in my faith walk (mid- to late 1990s) I started experiencing a nagging sense that I was supposed to do something for God. It kept gnawing at me inside and didn't go away. Though I had this feeling that I was supposed to do something for God, I didn't have the faintest idea what it was. In an effort to try to understand what it was I was supposed to do for God, I served on and then led a committee in my church and also served in a number of different ministries. Though all of these were good and enjoyable and somewhat fulfilling, not one of them felt like the right fit.

This all changed in the fall of 2002 during a worship service in which the preacher spoke about being ashamed of our relationship with Jesus. He looked at the congregation and emphatically stated, "Never be ashamed of your relationship with Jesus Christ!" I felt like he was speaking right to me. I knew I had been a closet Christian. I went right home and went down on my knees and apologized to God for being ashamed of my relationship with his Son. I immediately felt adrenaline surge throughout my whole body, and God, right then and there, gave me a directive regarding something he wanted me to do. He wanted me to lead a group in the church's small group ministry. I obeyed and he began guiding me, just like he guided the Israelites. He did not however, guide me with pillars of smoke and fire. He guided me by placing desires and passions in my heart.

The following spring (2003), a notice went out to all the small group leaders that the senior pastor was going to Saddleback Church in California to learn about a faith based recovery program called Celebrate Recovery. The notice included an open invitation for anyone who was interested to join him. I went, and while I was there, God finally let me know what it was he wanted me to do for him. He let me know that he wanted me to be a Celebrate Recovery Ministry Leader, and once again, I obeyed. When we got back to Pennsylvania, the church did decide to start a Celebrate Recovery Ministry and I did become the ministry leader.

What followed was one of the most difficult years of my life. Establishing and leading the Celebrate Recovery ministry was far harder than I ever imagined it would be. It was full of struggle, challenges, conflict, anger, hurt, fear, and self-doubt. Power battles abounded. My leadership was constantly challenged and undermined. God, however, continued to guide and direct me. He periodically reminded me that this was indeed what he wanted me to do in spite of what some human beings were saying.

One of the most powerful reminders came in spring '04 during a time in which I was particularly discouraged and full of doubt. One morning while I was praying, I asked God to show me what I needed to read or to hear and I opened my Bible. It opened to 1 Chronicles 28 (David commissioning Solomon to build the Temple). I started to read that chapter and the last two verses almost jumped off the page at me:

> Then David continued, "Be strong and courageous and do the work. Don't be afraid or discouraged by the size of the task, for the Lord God, my God, is with you. He will not fail you or forsake you. He will see to it that all the work related to the Temple of the Lord is finished correctly. The various divisions of priests and Levites will serve in the Temple of God. Others with skills of every kind will volunteer, and the leaders and the entire nation are at your command.
>
> 1 Chronicles 28:20–21

This confirmed to me that God did indeed want me to be a leader. I began to read those verses every day, sometimes multiple times in one day, and I slowly began to feel the burden of weight lifted off my shoulders. I knew that I wasn't alone. God was with me, smiling on me as I continued to obey him by leading this ministry. As I trusted that more and more, my faith became stronger and my fear decreased. My tendency to please people and seek their approval lessened and my commitment to live my life for an audience of One became stronger.

As I continued to lead the ministry, the challenges to my leadership and the power struggles intensified. I refused to give up because I knew I was walking in the will of God, doing what he wanted me to do. When I wouldn't step out of leadership on my own, others saw to it that my leadership of that ministry ended.

In November '04, I was removed from the position of Celebrate Recovery Ministry Leader by the pastors and some other leaders in the church. I was devastated and left my church. This was when God put me in a Crock-Pot.

Though my God-given purpose had been ripped away from me by human beings, I continued to sense God letting me know that he still wanted me to be a Celebrate Recovery leader. During this time, I was looking around for another church to join. I eventually found my way (or God led me) to a non-denominational church near my home. When the pastors of this church got to know me and understand the call God had placed on my life, they decided to start a Celebrate Recovery Ministry. I again stepped into the role of Celebrate Recovery Ministry Leader. We held our first meeting in April 2007.

While I was leading that ministry, God let me know that he no longer wanted me to work as a mental health professional as I had been doing for more than twenty years. Rather than obeying him though, I wrestled with him and tried to negotiate with him. He eventually grew tired of my disobedience and wrestling and made it next to impossible for me to stay in my profession. So in February 2008, I walked away from my career as a mental health professional and threw myself completely into Christ-centered recovery. That recovery ministry didn't last though. Sadly enough, the congregation and the community did not embrace

Celebrate Recovery and, due to lack of attendance, we decided to shut down the ministry in October 2008. The sense that God still wanted me to be a Celebrate Recovery leader did not leave me though.

God then led me to a Brethren in Christ Church, where I was asked to lead their Celebrate Recovery ministry. As I still sensed this call on my life from God, I agreed to lead their CR ministry. I led that ministry for four years until I no longer felt called to do so. I responded to this knowing by stepping out of leadership in September 2013, as I stated in the introduction. I then began a season of waiting.

What exactly it is I'm waiting for I don't know. All I know is that I do not have a clear directive from God right now as to what it is he wants me to do next. I do feel fairly certain though that God has another assignment for me. In order to be ready to effectively serve in whatever capacity God calls me to serve, I am using this time of waiting as a time of preparation. I am tending to some medical issues that I've been ignoring so that when God does let me know what he wants me to do next, I am in good physical health to do it.

God Smiles

Just as in the time of Noah and Moses, God smiles when we obey him. Our obedience unlocks the gate that holds his blessings and he then showers those blessings on us. By the same token, when we disobey him, he is displeased with us and he disciplines us. As stated in chapter 2, everything that God does for us he does out of love. He doesn't discipline us because he's angry at us or disappointed in us. He disciplines us because he loves us.

The word *discipline* comes from the same root as disciple, one who is taught. Therefore, when God is disciplining us, he is trying to teach us something. What is he teaching us? He is teaching us to be more like his Son. He is molding us, much like a potter molds clay, or chiseling away at us, much like a sculptor chisels a piece of stone. He is removing sinful behavior and replacing it with godly behavior.

For a wonderful visual image of this watch the Skit Guys video, *God's Chisel*, on Youtube: http://skitguys.com/videos/item/gods-chisel-2008.

During these times of disciplining, we would be well advised to cooperate with the work God is doing in us and accept the disciplining process. The following words of Moses to the people of Israel hold true for us today as well: "Think about it: Just as a parent disciplines a child, the Lord your God disciplines you for your own good" (Deuteronomy 8:5). It all comes back to knowing him and trusting him.

The blessing God showers on me when I obey him is an internal peace and joy that surpasses anything the world can give me. I have come to treasure this peace and joy. Because I treasure it so much, God takes it away from me when I disobey him. I am then filled with anxiety and depression and sadness. I am restless and agitated and feel anything but peaceful. This motivates me to get back on track with God and walk in his will for me. When I do this, he rewards me once again by showering his peace on me and filling me with it.

In summary, "When you come to a moment of truth when you must choose whether to obey God, you cannot obey Him unless you believe and trust Him. You cannot believe and trust Him, unless you love Him. You cannot love Him, unless you know Him."[2] Then the circle is unbroken.

Biblical Waiters

Two other biblical waiters we will take a look at are Moses and David, two of the most influential leaders in the Old Testament. Each had lengthy periods of waiting before stepping into the roles God wanted them to play.

Moses's Story

Moses was born in Egypt during the time that God's people were enslaved by the Egyptians. He was God's chosen individual to lead the Hebrews out of slavery in Egypt and bring them to the land God had promised Abraham long before that his descendants would occupy. He was the one who would make the following prophecy of Joseph's to his brothers come true, "God will surely come to help you and lead you out of this land of Egypt. He will bring you back to the land he solemnly promised to give to Abraham, to Isaac, and to Jacob" (Genesis 50:24).

The culture into which Moses was born is described in the first chapter of the book of Exodus.

> Eventually, a new king came to power in Egypt who knew nothing about Joseph or what he had done. He said to his people, "Look, the people of Israel now outnumber us and are stronger than we are. We must make a plan to keep them from growing even more. If we don't, and if war breaks out, they will join our enemies and fight against us. Then they will escape from the country." So the Egyptians made the Israelites their slaves. They appointed brutal slave drivers over them, hoping to wear them down with crushing labor. But the more the Egyptians oppressed them, the more the Israelites multiplied and spread, and the more alarmed the Egyptians became...Then Pharaoh, the king of Egypt, gave this order to the Hebrew midwives: "When you help the Hebrew women as they give birth, watch as they deliver. If the baby is a boy, kill him; if it is a girl, let her live." But because the midwives feared God, they refused to obey the king's orders. They allowed the boys to live too. Then Pharaoh gave this order to all his people: "Throw every newborn Hebrew boy into the Nile River. But you may let the girls live."
>
> Exodus 1:8–12, 15–17, 22

Because Moses was destined to play such a pivotal role in the story of God's people, God had his eye on Moses, protecting him from the moment of his birth.

When Doing Isn't Enough

The account of Moses's birth is told in the second chapter of the book of Exodus, verses 1–10.

> About this time, a man and woman from the tribe of Levi got married. The woman became pregnant and gave birth to a son. She saw that he was a special baby and kept him hidden for three months. But when she could no longer hide him, she got a basket made of papyrus reeds and waterproofed it with tar and pitch. She put the baby in the basket and laid it among the reeds along the bank of the Nile River. The baby's sister then stood at a distance, watching to see what would happen to him. Soon Pharaoh's daughter came down to bathe in the river, and her attendants walked along the riverbank. When the princess saw the basket among the reeds, she sent her maid to get it for her. When the princess opened it, she saw the baby. The little boy was crying, and she felt sorry for him.
>
> "This must be one of the Hebrew children," she said. Then the baby's sister approached the princess. "Should I go and find one of the Hebrew women to nurse the baby for you?" she asked. "Yes, do!" the princess replied. So the girl went and called the baby's mother. "Take this baby and nurse him for me," the princess told the baby's mother. "I will pay you for your help."
>
> So the woman took her baby home and nursed him. Later, when the boy was older, his mother brought him back to Pharaoh's daughter, who adopted him as her own son. The

princess named him Moses, for she explained, "I lifted him out of the water."

Exodus 2:1–10

There is no scriptural account of Moses's childhood or early adulthood. The next we hear of him he is forty years old and is killing an Egyptian because he witnessed the Egyptian beating a Hebrew. Moses then left Egypt because Pharaoh became aware of what Moses had done and tried to kill him. Several decades pass before we hear about Moses again. Moses is now eighty years old and working as a shepherd. God appears to him in a burning bush and communicates to him the special purpose God had chosen for him. "I am the God of your father—the God of Abraham, the God of Isaac, and the God of Jacob. The cry of the people of Israel has reached me, and I have seen how harshly the Egyptians abuse them. Now go, for I am sending you to Pharaoh. You must lead my people Israel out of Egypt" (Exodus 3:6, 9–10). Moses argued with God for a bit, trying to convince God that he had made a mistake and that he, Moses, was really not the best person to lead the Hebrews out of Egypt. As happens with any of us who have argued with God, Moses lost the argument. He eventually returned to Egypt to do what God had commanded him to do.

The first step in setting the Hebrew slaves free from their Egyptian masters was to convince the Hebrew people that he had actually been commissioned by God to lead them to freedom. God gave Moses the words to say to the Hebrews and empowered him to perform several miraculous signs to convince the Hebrews to follow him out of Egypt. God also assigned Moses's brother Aaron to help him by being Moses's spokesperson as Moses stuttered. Once the Hebrews were convinced that God truly had sent Moses to lead them out of Egypt, the next step was to convince Pharaoh to let the people go.

As he had done with the Hebrews, God told Moses and Aaron exactly what to say to Pharaoh and empowered them to perform many miraculous signs and wonders to convince Pharaoh that they were sent by God. As Pharaoh was extremely stubborn and hard-hearted, ten plagues were needed before Pharaoh agreed to let the Israelites leave Egypt. The plagues were progressively more destructive to the Egyptian people. (See Exodus 7:14–12:30). Pharaoh finally agreed to let the Hebrews leave Egypt. "Pharaoh sent for Moses and Aaron during the night. 'Get out!' he ordered. 'Leave my people—and take the rest of the Israelites with you! Go and worship the Lord as you have requested. Take your flocks and herds, as you said, and be gone. Go, but bless me as you leave'" (Exodus 12:31–32).

When the Israelites (about 600,000 men plus all the women and children) finally left Egypt, "God kept watch all night, watching over the Israelites as he brought them out of Egypt" (Exodus 12:41, MSG). God never left them. He continued to keep watch over them and lead them on their journey. "God went ahead of them in a Pillar of Cloud during the day to guide them on the way, and at night in a Pillar of Fire to give them light; thus they could travel both day and night. The

Pillar of Cloud by day and the Pillar of Fire by night never left the people" (Exodus 13:21–22, MSG). God continued to provide the Israelites with miraculous signs as they continued on their journey. (See Exodus 14:5–31.)

When the Israelites arrived at the land of Canaan, Moses, per God's direction, sent out a small group of men to scout out the land. After forty days, they returned and gave the following report to Moses and all the Israelites:

> We went to the land to which you sent us and, oh! It does flow with milk and honey! Just look at this fruit! The only thing is that the people who live there are fierce, their cities are huge and well-fortified. Worse yet, we saw descendants of the giant Anak. Amalekites are spread out in the Negev; Hittites, Jebusites, and Amorites hold the hill country; and the Canaanites are established on the Mediterranean Sea and along the Jordan.
>
> Numbers 13:27–29 (MSG)

One of the members of the scouting party, Caleb, urged the people of Israel to move forward and take the land. The others in the scouting party, however, discouraged this, saying: "It's a land that swallows people whole. Everybody we saw was huge…Alongside them we felt like grasshoppers. And they looked down on us as if we were grasshoppers" (Numbers 13:32–33, MSG). When the people of Israel heard this, the whole community erupted in weeping and wailing. They then rebelled against Moses and Aaron and began planning to choose a new leader.

Caleb, along with Joshua, another member of the scouting party, stepped forward and addressed the entire community of Israel, saying:

> The land we walked through and scouted is a very good land—very good indeed. If God is pleased with us, he will lead us into that land, a land that flows, as they say, with milk and honey. And he'll give it to us. Just don't rebel against God! And don't be afraid of those people. Why, we'll have them for lunch! They have no protection and God is on our side. Don't be afraid of them!
>
> Numbers 14:7–9 (MSG)

The people reacted to Joshua's and Caleb's statements by threatening to stone them. God then appeared to Moses and said, "How long will these people treat me like dirt? How long refuse to trust me? And with all these signs I've done among them!" (Numbers 14:11, MSG) After a fairly long interchange between God and Moses in which Moses interceded for the people of Israel, God instructed Moses to give the following message to the Israelites:

> Your children, the very ones that you said would be taken for plunder, I'll bring in to enjoy the land you rejected while your corpses will be rotting in the wilderness. These children of yours will live as shepherds in the wilderness for forty years,… You scouted out the land for

> forty days; your punishment will be a year for each day, a forty-year sentence to serve for your sins—a long schooling in my displeasure.
>
> Numbers 14:31–34 (MSG)

Throughout the long, difficult years in the wilderness, Moses trusted God and God never abandoned him. God guided him and directed him as to what to do and when to do it. Each time the people complained and rebelled and disobeyed and God became angry with them, Moses intervened for the people and God listened to him.

When they reached the promised land for the second and final time, Moses didn't actually lead the people into the land. Joshua did that. When God told Moses that he was about to die, Moses, per God's instruction, commissioned Joshua to be his successor. (See Numbers 27:12–23.) Moses then spoke to the people of Israel, saying, "I am now 120 years old, and I am no longer able to lead you. The Lord has told me, 'You will not cross the Jordan River.' But the Lord your God himself will cross over ahead of you. He will destroy the nations living there, and you will take possession of their land. Joshua will lead you across the river, just as the Lord promised" (Deuteronomy 31:2–3).

As Joseph had before him, Moses continued to trust in God and God's plan for himself and for the people of Israel.

> Then Moses went up to Mount Nebo from the plains of Moab and climbed Pisgah Peak, which is across from Jericho. And the Lord showed

him the whole land... Then the Lord said to Moses, "This is the land I promised on oath to Abraham, Isaac, and Jacob when I said, 'I will give it to your descendants.' I have now allowed you to see it with your own eyes, but you will not enter the land." So Moses, the servant of the Lord, died there in the land of Moab, just as the Lord had said.

Deuteronomy 34:1, 4–5

Scripture then goes on to tell us, "There has never been another prophet in Israel like Moses, whom the Lord knew face to face. The Lord sent him to perform all the miraculous signs and wonders in the land of Egypt against Pharaoh, and all his servants, and his entire land. With mighty power, Moses performed terrifying acts in the sight of all Israel" (Deuteronomy 34:10–12).

It is important to remember that the "mighty power" Moses displayed was not his own power. It was God's power flowing through him. It is absolutely amazing what God can do through an ordinary human being who trusts him, has waited on him, and has totally surrendered himself or herself to him.

Something to Think About

Moses was eighty years old when God revealed to him the special purpose God had chosen for him. Why do you think God timed it this way? Maybe because Moses needed to simmer in a Crock-Pot for that long so he was adequately prepared to effectively accomplish the unbelievably huge task of leading 600,000 plus individuals out of captivity in Egypt with the Egyptian army on their heels, only to reach their destination and have the people refuse to enter the land, and then continue to lead them as they wandered in the wilderness for forty years. Skill and technique would not have carried Moses the distance in accomplishing this. Only character and a strong, trusting relationship with God would do that. Moses evidently needed to simmer for a long time so his character could be formed and his relationship with God could be developed to the point that he could do what God, the potter and the sculptor, asked him to do.

Something Else to Think About

Can you imagine how Moses must have felt when the scouts returned from scouting out the land of Canaan and the people reacted with fear and refused to keep moving forward? Their mistrust of God after all God had done for them (the ten plagues, parting the Red Sea so they could get away from the Egyptian army, drowning the Egyptians in the Red Sea, guiding them with a Pillar of Fire and a Pillar of Cloud, and providing quail and bread and water so they wouldn't die of thirst or starvation) must have been extremely frustrating for him. Moses, however, didn't throw up his hands in disgust and walk away from the people of Israel. Instead, he accepted the punishment God meted out on the people for their refusal to trust him and continued to lead the people of Israel for another *forty years* dealing with all their grumbling, rebellion, blame, and coup attempts.

One of the incidents which occurred during that forty-year period is described in the book of Numbers 21:4–5.

> Then the people of Israel set out from Mount Hor, taking the road to the Red Sea to go around the land of Edom. But the people grew impatient with the long journey, and they began to speak against God and Moses. "Why have you brought us out of Egypt to die here in the wilderness?" they complained. "There is nothing to eat here and nothing to drink. And we hate this horrible manna!"

Take note, this is only one of who knows how many such incidents Moses had to deal with during that forty-year period. No wonder he had to simmer for a long time!

Moses died approximately 1406 or 1405 BC as the people of Israel were on the verge of entering the Promised Land.

When the Israelites entered the Promised Land, they were faced with many walled cities full of enemies. The Israelites, led by Joshua, captured each of the enemy cities one by one. Eventually, the Israelites overcame all their enemies and possessed the land, settling into their lives in the land God had promised them long before.

After Joshua died, the people were led by a series of prophets and judges who were all godly leaders. The word translated "judged" (shapat) combines the ideas of "national leadership," "judicial decisions," and "political, military savior." The people of Israel eventually grew tired of this style of leadership and asked to have a king so they could be like the nations around them. This occurred toward the end of the life of Samuel, the prophet.

> As Samuel grew old, he appointed his sons to be judges over Israel. Joel and Abijah, his oldest sons, held court in Beersheba. But they were not like their father, for they were greedy for money. They accepted bribes and perverted justice. Finally, all the elders of Israel met at Ramah to discuss the matter with Samuel. "Look," they told him, "you are now old, and your sons are not like you. Give us a king to judge us like all the other nations have." Samuel was displeased with their request and went to the Lord for guidance. "Do everything they say to you," the Lord replied, "for it is me they are rejecting, not you. They don't want me to be their king any longer. Ever since I brought them from Egypt they have continually abandoned me and followed other gods. And now they are giving you the same treatment. Do as they ask."
>
> 1 Samuel 8:1–9

The first king of Israel was Saul. David was the second.

David's Story

David lived approximately 200 years after Moses. The first we hear of David he is a young boy tending his father's sheep.

God had become dissatisfied with the way Saul was leading as king and communicated this to Samuel. "Now the Lord said to Samuel, 'You have mourned long enough for Saul. I have rejected him as king of Israel, so fill your flask with olive oil and go to Bethlehem. Find a man named Jesse who lives there, for I have selected one of his sons to be my new king'" (1 Samuel 16:1).

When Samuel arrived at Jesse's home, David was not even called in from the fields to meet him as David was still a boy. Samuel met David's seven older brothers; however, God made it clear to Samuel that he had not chosen any of these men to be his king. When David was finally called in from the fields, God let Samuel know that David was the one he had chosen to be the next king of Israel. "So as David stood there among his brothers, Samuel took the flask of olive oil he had brought and anointed David with the oil. And the Spirit of the Lord came powerfully upon David from that day on. Then Samuel returned to Ramah" (1 Samuel 16:13).

And David waited to become king.

The next we hear of David he is called to Saul's court to serve him.

> Now the Spirit of the Lord had left Saul, and the Lord sent a tormenting spirit that filled him with depression and fear. Some of Saul's servant's said to him, "A tormenting spirit from God is troubling you. Let us find a good musician to play the harp whenever the tormenting spirit troubles you. He will play soothing music, and you will soon be well

again." "All right," Saul said. "Find me someone who plays well, and bring him here." One of the servants said to Saul, "One of Jesse's sons from Bethlehem is a talented harp player. Not only that—he is a brave warrior, a man of war, and has good judgment. He is also a fine-looking young man, and the Lord is with him." So Saul sent messengers to Jesse to say, "Send me your son David, the shepherd." Jesse responded by sending David to Saul, along with a young goat, a donkey loaded with bread, and a wineskin full of wine. So David went to Saul and began serving him. Saul loved David very much, and David became his armor bearer. Then Saul sent word to Jesse asking, "Please let David remain in my service, for I am very pleased with him." And whenever the tormenting spirit from God troubled Saul, David would play the harp. Then Saul would feel better, and the tormenting spirit would go away.

1 Samuel 16:14–23

And David waited to become king.

During this time, Israel was at war with the Philistines, one of the enemy nations surrounding them. At one point, the two armies were encamped on two hills facing each other with a valley in between them.

> Then Goliath, a Philistine champion from Gath, came out of the Philistine ranks to face the forces of Israel. He was over nine feet tall! He wore a bronze helmet, and his bronze coat of mail weighed 125 pounds. He also wore bronze leg armor, and he carried a bronze javelin on

his shoulder. The shaft of his spear was as heavy and thick as a weaver's beam, tipped with an iron spearhead that weighed 15 pounds. His armor bearer walked ahead of him carrying a shield. Goliath stood and shouted a taunt across to the Israelites. "Why are you all coming out to fight?" he called. "I am the Philistine champion, but you are only the servants of Saul. Choose one man to come down here and fight me! If he kills me, then we will be your slaves. But if I kill him, you will be our slaves! I defy the armies of Israel today! Send me a man who will fight me!" When Saul and the Israelites heard this, they were terrified and deeply shaken.

> 1 Samuel 17:4–11

"For forty days, every morning and evening, the Philistine champion strutted in front of the Israelite army" (1 Samuel 17:16). One day, David was at the battlefield and heard Goliath taunt the Israelites. His reaction to this was to ask one of the soldiers, "Who is this pagan Philistine anyway, that he is allowed to defy the armies of the living God?" (1 Samuel 17:26). Saul learned of what David had said and sent for him.

> "Don't worry about this Philistine," David told Saul. "I'll go fight him!" "Don't be ridiculous!" Saul replied. "There's no way you can fight this Philistine and possibly win! You're only a boy, and he's been a man of war since his youth."
>
> But David persisted. "I have been taking care of my father's sheep and goats," he said. "When a lion or a bear comes to steal a lamb

from the flock, I go after it with a club and rescue the lamb from its mouth. If the animal turns on me, I catch it by the jaw and club it to death. I have done this to both lions and bears, and I'll do it to this pagan Philistine, too, for he has defied the armies of the living God! The Lord who rescued me from the claws of the lion and the bear will rescue me from this Philistine!"...

He picked up five smooth stones from a stream and put them into his shepherd's bag. Then, armed only with the shepherd's staff and sling, he started across the valley to fight the Philistine....

David replied to the Philistine, "You come to me with sword, spear, and javelin, but I come to you in the name of the Lord of Heaven's Armies–the God of the armies of Israel, whom you have defied. Today the Lord will conquer you, and I will kill you and cut off your head. And then I will give the dead bodies of your men to the birds and wild animals, and the whole world will know that there is a God in Israel! And everyone assembled here will know that the Lord rescues his people, but not with sword and spear. This is the Lord's battle, and he will give you to us!"

As Goliath moved closer to attack, David quickly ran out to meet him. Reaching into his shepherd's bag and taking out a stone, he hurled it with his sling and hit the Philistine in the forehead. The stone sank in, and Goliath stumbled and fell face down on the ground.

> So David triumphed over the Philistine with only a sling and a stone, for he had no sword. Then David ran over and pulled Goliath's sword from its sheath. David used it to kill him and cut off his head.
>
> 1 Samuel 17:32–37, 40, 45–51a

"From that day on Saul kept David with him and wouldn't let David return home" (1 Samuel 18:2). "Whatever Saul asked David to do, David did it successfully. So Saul made him a commander over the men of war, an appointment that was welcomed by the people and Saul's officers alike" (1 Samuel 18:5).

Saul soon became jealous of David and felt threatened by him. He tried to kill David twice with his spear, but David got away from him both times. Saul's jealousy and fear of David went from bad to worse and he tried several more times to kill David. All of the attempts were unsuccessful. David survived each time. Saul's son Jonathan, who was David's best friend, and Saul's daughter Michal, who was David's wife, both helped him with some of his escapes. Like Joseph before him, David had done nothing wrong to merit these attempts on his life.

And David waited to become king.

Though Saul had tried many times to kill David, David did not retaliate in kind when two opportunities presented themselves for him to kill Saul. See 1 Samuel 24:1–22 and 1 Samuel 26:1–25.

Over the course of the years that David was fleeing from Saul, many fighting men joined him until David was eventually the leader of a small army. "So David left Gath and escaped to the cave of Adullam. Soon his brothers and all his other relatives joined him there. Then others began coming—men who were in trouble or in debt or who were just discontented—until David was the captain of about 400 men" (1 Samuel 22:1–2). "Some brave and experienced warriors from the tribe of Gad also defected to David while he was at the stronghold in the wilderness. They were expert with both shield and spear, as fierce as lions and as swift as deer on the mountains" (1 Chronicles 12:8).

Over time, David and his men earned a reputation as fierce warriors. All this time, Israel was at war with Philistine. Eventually, Saul and three of his sons were killed in battle, all on the same day.

One of Saul's soldiers went to David and told him of Saul's death.

> After this, David asked the Lord, "Should I move back to one of the towns of Judah?" "Yes," the Lord replied. Then David asked, "Which town should I go to?" "To Hebron," the Lord answered. So David and his wives and his men and their families all moved to Judah, and they settled in the villages near Hebron. Then the men of Judah came to David and anointed him king over the people of Judah.
>
> 2 Samuel 2:1–4

One of Saul's sons, Ishbosheth, also became king. "That was the beginning of a long war between those who were loyal to Saul and those loyal to David. As time passed David became stronger and stronger, while

Saul's dynasty became weaker and weaker" (2 Samuel 3:1). Ishbosheth was then murdered by two of his own warriors. "Then all the tribes of Israel went to David at Hebron and told him, 'We are your own flesh and blood. In the past, when Saul was our king, you were the one who really led the forces of Israel. And the Lord told you, 'You will be the shepherd of my people Israel. You will be Israel's leader'" (2 Samuel 5:1–2). "So there at Hebron, David made a covenant before the Lord with all the elders of Israel. And they anointed him king of Israel, just as the Lord had promised through Samuel" (1 Chronicles 11:3).

So after all David's years of waiting, all that time simmering in a slow-cooker, David was finally king over the entire nation of Israel.

Soon after David became king, he and his warriors engaged the Philistine army in battle and conquered them. "So David's fame spread everywhere, and the Lord caused all the nations to fear David" (1 Chronicles 14:17). David and his men then initiated an attack against the Jebusites, who were occupying the city of Jerusalem. They captured the city and David made his home there, renaming it the City of David. "And David became more and more powerful, because the Lord God of Heaven's Armies was with him" (2 Samuel 5:10).

"David was thirty years old when he began to reign, and he reigned forty years in all. He had reigned over Judah from Hebron for seven years and six months, and from Jerusalem he reigned over all Israel and Judah for thirty-three years" (2 Samuel 5:4–5).

Though David clearly carried God's anointing to be king and had waited and simmered for a long time before becoming king, he was still human and his humanity was clearly evident in his kingship. It is important to remember that though someone may be anointed by God to lead, that individual is still human and, therefore, not perfect. He or she will make mistakes and will have flaws. The mistakes and the flaws do not cancel out the divine anointing, and the anointing does not remove all traces of an imperfect human nature.

David did many very good things as king. He also did some very bad things as king.

Good things:

1. He returned the Ark of the Covenant to a place of honor in Jerusalem. The story of the Ark is told in Exodus 40, Joshua 3 and 4, 1 Samuel 4:1–7:2, and 2 Samuel 6:1–15.

2. He had many military victories over enemy nations surrounding Israel. "The Lord made David victorious wherever he went" (1 Chronicles 18:13).

3. He dedicated the plunder he collected after each victory to the Lord. "King David dedicated all these gifts to the Lord, as he did with the silver and gold from the other nations he had defeated" (2 Samuel 8:11).

4. He brought Mephibosheth, a crippled son of Jonathan's and a grandson of Saul's, to his palace and included him in his own family, treating him like a son.

When Doing Isn't Enough

Bad thing:

He impregnated Bathsheba, the wife of Uriah, one of his officers, and then arranged to have Uriah killed. See 2 Samuel 11:1–24.

Following Uriah's death God sent the prophet Nathan to confront David about his sinful behavior. David's response was to repent for what he had done.

Good thing:

He repented of his sinful behavior regarding Bathsheba and Uriah.

Important Note: Though David repented, he still experienced the consequences of his actions. Repentance gets us right with God; however, it does not erase the occurrence of consequences.

Nathan communicated to David what God had deemed appropriate consequences for his actions.

> This is what the Lord says: "Because of what you have done, I will cause your own household to rebel against you. I will give your wives to another man before your very eyes, and he will go to bed with them in public view. You did it secretly, but I will make this happen to you openly in the sight of all Israel…the Lord has forgiven you, and you won't die for this sin. Nevertheless, because you have shown utter contempt for the Lord by doing this, your child will die."
>
> 2 Samuel 12:11–14

The child born as a result of David forcing himself on Bathsheba while Uriah was alive did indeed die. This was not the end of David and Bathsheba's relationship though. The story of their relationship is told in 2 Samuel 11:2–12 and 25; 1 Kings 1:11–31; and 1 Kings 2:13–21

Bad thing:

David failed to deal directly with his daughter's rape.

David had many sons and daughters from a variety of wives and concubines. One of David's sons, Amnon, raped his half-sister, Tamar, one of David's daughters. Following the rape, Tamar went to live with her full brother, Absalom.

When King David heard about what had happened he was very angry. And though Absalom never spoke to Amnon about this, he hated Amnon deeply because of what he had done to his sister. Two years later Absalom had Amnon killed. One of David's nephews told David "Absalom has been plotting this ever since Amnon raped his sister Tamar" 2 (Samuel 13:32).

Absalom then left Jerusalem and went to live in a foreign land. After three years Absalom returned to Jerusalem with David's blessing however David refused to see him. Two years later David finally agreed to let Absalom come into his presence and they were reconciled. Four years after that though Absalom stirred up a rebellion against his father, King David. "Soon many others also joined Absalom, and the conspiracy gained momentum" (2 Samuel 15:12).

When Doing Isn't Enough

When David learned of this, he left Jerusalem and Absalom took up residence in the king's palace. In the midst of this, David continued to trust God.

> Everyone cried loudly as the king and his followers passed by. They crossed the Kidron Valley and then went out toward the wilderness. Zadok and all the Levites also came along, carrying the Ark of the Covenant of God. They set down the Ark of God, and Abiathar offered sacrifices until everyone had passed out of the city. Then the king instructed Zadok to take the Ark of God back into the city. "If the Lord sees fit," David said, "he will bring me back to see the Ark and the Tabernacle again. But if he is through with me, then let him do what seems best to him."
>
> 2 Samuel 15:23–26

Eventually the Israelite army, led by Absalom, met David's warriors on the field of battle.

> So the battle began in the forest of Ephraim, and the Israelite troops were beaten back by David's men. There was a great slaughter that day, and 20,000 men laid down their lives... During the battle, Absalom happened to come upon some of David's men. He tried to escape on his mule, but as he rode beneath the thick branches of a great tree, his hair got caught in the tree. His mule kept going and left him dangling in the air... he (Joab, one of David's officers) took three daggers and plunged them into Absalom's heart as he dangled, still alive, in

the great tree. Ten of Joab's young armor bearers then surrounded Absalom and killed him.

2 Samuel 18:6, 9, 14–15

And throughout all the tribes of Israel there was much discussion and argument going on. The people were saying, "The king rescued us from our enemies and saved us from the Philistines, but Absalom chased him out of the country. Now Absalom, whom we anointed to rule over us, is dead. Why not ask David to come back and be our king again?

2 Samuel 19:9–10

So David returned to Jerusalem and once again became the king of Israel.

In summary, David's sinful behavior with Bathsheba and Uriah and his failure to deal directly with Amnon for raping Tamar led to Absalom taking matters into his own hands and killing Amnon and then leading the successful revolt against David. All of Nathan's prophecies came true. David's household rebelled against him and his wives were given to another man who went to bed with them in public view. When Absalom moved into his father's palace, "they set up a tent on the palace roof where everyone could see it, and Absalom went in and had sex with his father's concubines" (2 Samuel 16:22).

There is a time to wait and a time to act. "For everything there is a season, a time for every activity under heaven...A time to tear and a time to mend. A time to be quiet and a time to speak" (Ecclesiastes 3:1, 7).

When Doing Isn't Enough

David's last act as king was a very good one. He made all the preparations for a temple to be built to the Lord. He made sure everything was in place. He then delegated this task to his son Solomon.

> David summoned all the officials of Israel to Jerusalem—the leaders of the tribes, the commanders of the army divisions, the other generals and captains, the overseers of the royal property and livestock, the palace officials, the mighty men and all the other brave warriors in the kingdom. David rose to his feet and said: "My brothers and my people! It was my desire to build a temple where the Ark of the Lord's Covenant, God's footstool, could rest permanently. I made the necessary preparations for building it, but God said to me, 'You must not build a temple to honor my name, for you are a warrior and have shed much blood.'... And from among my sons—for the Lord has given me many—he chose Solomon to succeed me on the throne of Israel and to rule over the Lord's kingdom. He said to me, 'Your son Solomon will build my Temple and its courtyards, for I have chosen him as my son, and I will be his father.'"
>
> 1 Chronicles 28:1–3, 5–6

"Then David died and was buried with his ancestors in the City of David. Solomon became king and sat on the throne of David his father, and his kingdom was firmly established" (1 Kings 2:10, 12).

Twenty-First Century Waiters

God still asks people to wait on him, just as he did in biblical times. Some individuals make a conscious decision to wait on God. Others find themselves in a Crock-Pot where they have little choice but to wait on God. Julia chose to wait on God. Brian found himself in a Crock-Pot, as did Dave and Amy (different Amy).

Julia's Story

Julia grew up as the youngest of four children with Christian parents in a strong Bible-believing church. One Sunday when she was six years old, her mother asked her what she learned in Sunday school that day. Julia's answer was that she learned that Jesus could live inside our hearts. Her mother then asked her if she would like to ask Jesus into her heart. She said yes. Her mother and sister prayed with her and she did ask Jesus to come into her heart. She was baptized at age ten and has been a Christ follower ever since. Julia stated that she can't remember a time in her life that she didn't know Jesus and can't imagine not having Jesus in her life.

Julia also stated that from a very young age all she wanted in life was to be a wife and mother. She can't remember a time in her life when she did not want this. She stated, "I knew it was my calling" and "I couldn't imagine not being a wife and mother."

Due to the example her parents and older siblings set, she grew up knowing what to look for in a husband. That husband, however, did not come into her life until she was in her late twenties. Throughout her early adulthood, she dated and had relationships with men. None of the men she was involved with, however, matched the picture of a godly husband she had developed during her childhood.

Two of her siblings each married when they were nineteen. In addition, when Julia was in her early twenties, almost all her close Christian girlfriends got married. As the years went by, most of them had a child and were expecting their second child and Julia was still waiting for a husband. Though she was happy for them, she couldn't help but be sad for herself and wonder why it was taking so long for her to have a family of her own. Though she wondered this and felt discouraged at times, she never lost hope that there was a man out there for her and trusted that the Lord would bring him to her when the time was right. She held on to that hope by holding on to the following scripture verse: "Delight yourself in the Lord and he will give you the desires of your heart" (Psalm 37:4 NIV).

Then one Sunday, her brother invited her to attend his church. While she was there, her brother introduced her to a single man. Upon meeting him, Julia didn't feel any immediate interest in him. However, she did begin to attend her brother's church regularly. It was during the following weeks that she began to notice this man through his consistently friendly, happy, and outgoing nature. She also began hearing good things about him from other people and observed for herself that he had a caring servant's heart toward people. Her opinion of him gradually changed and she began to take an interest in him. He, however, was not showing any signs of interest in her. While he would greet her weekly with a smile and a hello, there was little other communication from him.

About one month later, Julia was driving home from church one Sunday. She was feeling discouraged that God wasn't bringing a man into her life and she was crying. She began to pray about it and this man's name came into her mind. She kept praying and "couldn't shake" his name out of her mind. Over the next few months, she kept praying about it and "giving it to the Lord." She stated that she wanted a man who would be the "spiritual leader" of the couple and due to this she knew that "he would have to see it too" and pursue her. She also stated that she did not want to take matters into her own hands. She wanted God to do it, so she kept praying.

About four months later, this man shared his testimony at church and this solidified her interest in him. Though he was still not expressing any interest in her, she "never lost hope" that he would pursue her. A few weeks later, he asked her out, and one year later, almost to the day, they were married.

Once they began dating, he explained to her that he was unable to ask her out any earlier than he did due to a situation in his life that he was dealing with. If she had taken matters into her own hands, she may have sabotaged any chance of a relationship with him. This confirmed to her that God did indeed know what was best for her and she would never go wrong to wait on him.

At the time of this writing, Julia has been happily married for two years and is the mother of a healthy, handsome son.

Brian's Story

Brian grew up in a Christian family in Ohio. His family attended a church where he heard "lots of fire and brimstone" preached. Brian stated that even as a young child, he experienced "a pervasive sense that I needed the salvation they kept talking about." So one Sunday, when he was six years old, he nudged his parents in church and told them he wanted to go forward and be saved. His parents responded by saying, "Wait, let's talk about this." When they got home, his parents reiterated the salvation message to him, and he said, "Yes, I get it and I want it." So at six years old, Brian gave his life to Christ in the family's living room.

When he was thirteen, the family moved to Pennsylvania and again became involved in a local church. It was here that Brian learned to personalize his faith through involvement in the church's youth group. The youth group was led by a "dynamic" youth pastor with a heart for missions. He took the teenagers "all over the place" on various mission trips and the "seeds of ministry were planted" in Brian's heart.

When he graduated from high school, Brian went to a Bible college to study for the ministry and to prepare to do missions work. After one and a half years in Bible college, Brian began to feel that ministry/missions was the "last thing" he wanted to do. Though Brian had given his life to Christ and felt that "the seeds of ministry" had been planted in his heart, he struggled with turning full control of his life over to God. So not fully knowing what God was calling him to and not desiring any type of ministry role, he left college and joined the Marine Corps. He served in the Marine Corps for five years. During this time, he married a young woman he had met in his youth group. While he was in the military, his relationship with God was "not a priority" and he "put it on a back shelf." Brian left the Marine Corps in 1996 and finished college on the GI bill. He then got a job at a pharmaceutical company. "With that came a house and a baby."

After about five years working in the corporate world, Brian "realized the emptiness" of living a life based primarily on the pursuit of the American dream of acquiring more and bigger "stuff" and, once again, made his relationship with God a priority. He "started asking bigger life questions" such as "what is God's agenda for my life?" He felt a stirring in his heart which led him to believe that God was "calling" him to do something else. The seeds of ministry and mission work which God had planted in his heart when he was a teenager began to sprout. By this time, Brian's trust in Christ had developed to the point that he was more willing to abide by God's plan for his life rather than his own, and he and his wife felt called to respond to this stirring by joining a missions organization which focused on church planting. After a lengthy training process, they moved to South America to join a church planting team.

The "biblical model" he followed for leaving the United States and settling in a foreign country was Abraham. "The Lord had said to Abram, 'Leave your native country, your relatives, and your father's family, and go to the land that I will show you'" (Genesis 12:1).

When Brian and his wife joined this missionary team and moved to South America, they committed to serve for two years, though in their minds they really believed they would be there much longer. The reality of their experience in South America, however, wasn't at all what they had anticipated it would be. The challenges they encountered there proved to be too much for their young family (they had another baby while in South America) and they came back to the United States in July 2006 after having been in South America for three years.

Brian described his return to the United States as "very disorienting." He had no job, no income, and didn't know what he was going to do next. He soon found himself in a Crock-Pot where he had little choice but to wait on God. He began to question and doubt the trust he had developed in God, and his willingness to put his life completely in God's hands evaporated. His description of his time in the Crock-Pot was that it was "hard" as he "was not in control" of his life. He stated that he was "angry with God" because they were "beyond strapped financially" and he couldn't understand why God would put them in that desperate position.

After spending approximately ten months in a Crock-Pot, Brian once again got a job in the corporate world. When he got this job, Brian vowed that he would *never* go back to having to trust God again.

Looking back on this time in his life, Brian realized that God had put him in that Crock-Pot because there was a "huge lesson" he needed to learn. That lesson regarded how he viewed and measured success. Brian's time in the Crock-Pot resulted in him changing his definition of success from achieving results and acquiring "stuff" to "obeying God."

Brian also eventually came to truly believe that God was doing things he "couldn't see" and that "God was working out a plan" for his life. He eventually realized and accepted as truth that "God was in control" of his life and that was okay. This realization came during an "aha moment" he experienced while listening to a sermon on the life of Joseph. The following words of Joseph to his brothers cemented these lessons into Brian's mind and heart. "You intended to harm me, but God intended it all for good" (Genesis 50:20). Joseph then became Brian's "biblical model" for his return to the United States and Brian shifted control of his life from his hands back into God's hands, believing they were better hands for his life to be in.

God was still not finished with Brian so he continued to poke at him and nudge him. About two to three years into this second corporate job, God began to remind Brian of the seeds of ministry he had planted in Brian's heart as a teenager and which had begun to sprout during his first corporate job. Those plants now grew taller and stronger. Brian's heart "moved away from the job" and he began "feeling pulled back to ministry." Brian responded to this by "every now and then" doing employment searches for open ministry positions. During one of these searches, he saw a posting for a position of Director of Spiritual Formation at a nearby church. He applied for the position, was called in for an interview, and was hired. So in April 2011, Brian once again left the corporate world and stepped into the world of ministry. As he did this, he saw with clarity how God had been working in his life all along. His time in the corporate world had been a necessary part of his preparation process as both corporate jobs had taught him skills he would need to effectively accomplish the responsibilities of the ministry role he was stepping into.

As Brian reflected on his spiritual journey to date, he stated that his learning has evolved into a deeper and wider understanding of what it truly means to give your life to Christ. He now understands that God was weaving a bigger story in those moments where the individual pieces of the story seemed to make no sense from his immediate vantage point. Even in the moments when Brian was wrestling with questions of control, God was teaching him priceless lessons that, today, help him shepherd those who are wrestling with those very same questions.

At the time of this writing, Brian is continuing to serve in ministry in the same church body. He doesn't know if he will be doing this for two months or two years or twenty years. He doesn't know if God wants him to stay there or if God has something he wants Brian to do somewhere else. However, he is open to whatever God has for him knowing that "God's got it" and that's okay.

Dave and Amy's Story

Dave was born and raised in suburban Philadelphia in a "stable, Christian home." His father supported the family through his employment as a diesel mechanic, and his mother was a stay-at-home mom. The family attended and was actively involved in an independent, non-denominational, Bible-believing church. His father was a deacon in the church and later became an elder. His mother taught Sunday school for the four- and five-year-old children. In speaking of his parent's and extended family's church involvement, Dave stated that he always had "a pretty good legacy of faith."

Dave reported that his mother led him to the Lord when he was five years old. He asked her to do this sensing that he was a naughty little guy who needed to be saved. She read *The Wordless Book* with him and talked with him about the salvation plan until she was satisfied that he truly understood it. He then prayed the sinner's prayer and asked Jesus to be his Lord and Savior.

Three years later, when he was in third grade, he was involved in an accident in which he seriously injured his arm, cutting it down to the bone and losing much blood. He spent one week in the hospital in an intensive care unit receiving massive blood transfusions and many, many stitches on multiple layers of his arm. Dave stated that this experience was a "turning point" for him in that, while he was in the hospital, he had "conversations with God" in which he asked God why his life had been spared. He realized that three years earlier, God had saved him from spiritual death and had now saved him from physical death. This resulted in him feeling that he had to make his life "count." Dave knew that he had been blessed with "musical gifts" and he began to take "a serious look" at these musical gifts.

Throughout middle school and high school, Dave was greatly influenced by the youth pastor in his church who challenged him to stand up for his faith and turn away from sin. The youth pastor led Dave through a one-on-one discipleship program. While in high school Dave, "turned another corner." His commitment to Christ deepened and his resolve to live for Christ took root in him. He felt like he "stood for something" and was outspoken in his faith. He was part of a Christian rap group that performed at local youth rallies and events. The group disbanded when they graduated in 1994 as they were all heading in different directions. While in high school, he also met and started dating a girl named Amy.

Amy was also born and raised in suburban Philadelphia, in a neighboring town to Dave. They met at a church event, a concert that they each attended with their youth group.

Amy was the youngest of four children in a two-parent home. All of her siblings were teenagers when she was born. Growing up, she felt like an only child in some ways as she and her parents did many things together just the three of them while her siblings were off being teenagers.

Amy's parents were also Christian and actively involved in a local Baptist church. The summer before Amy entered sixth grade, she broke her arm. This resulted in her spending much time inside that summer. Prior to this, she had been going to middle school church events. Her hiatus from summer activities gave her time to think about what she had been learning in church. She realized this was "serious stuff" and decided that summer to give her life to Christ. Throughout the rest of middle school and high school, she stayed involved with her church youth group as well as participating in Christian events at her high school.

Following Dave's graduation from high school, he became part of a musical ministry called Carpenter's Tools International. He traveled with them to Africa, Hungary, the Dominican Republic, and Canada, as well as touring the United States. He stated that this experience was "life-changing" in that he "saw people come to Christ" and/or "rededicate their lives to Christ," seeing first-hand the "hunger" in people for the divine. He was also away from Amy for fourteen months.

As Amy was a year behind Dave in school, he was away for her entire senior year. Though they "kept the relationship going long distance" this was a "very hard" year for Amy as she had become "very attached" to Dave. When Dave came home, they each realized that they were very committed to each other and to the relationship, and they became engaged soon after his return home. They then went off together to a small Christian college in Tennessee as an engaged couple. They married two years later, in 1997, and moved into married students housing.

Though Dave and Amy knew from the beginning of their marriage that they wanted a family, they also knew that they both wanted to graduate from college and knew that a baby would make this difficult. So, for the first two years of their marriage, they took steps to prevent this from happening. When they graduated from college in '99 (he with a bachelor's degree in music, and she with a bachelor's degree in biology) however, they stopped using birth control. They put pregnancy "in God's hands" as they each furthered their careers. They moved to Nashville where Dave earned a second bachelor's degree in audio engineering from Middle Tennessee State University while Amy worked in a pharmacy. Amy described this as a "lonely time" for her as Dave was "working insane hours" and she "didn't know anybody." She also stated that, while in Nashville, "the long winding road that God took me on" ended.

While in high school and then throughout college, she worked in a pharmacy and "loved it." She didn't think she could be a pharmacist though because all the

When Doing Isn't Enough

pharmacists she had ever known were older men. In Nashville, she worked with a young female pharmacist who was in her thirties and for the first time in her life, Amy began to believe that it was possible for a woman to be a pharmacist. In addition to the encouragement that she received from this pharmacist, God pinned her to the wall and let her know that this is what he wanted her to do and he would see her through. So, when Dave graduated, they moved back to Philadelphia where she attended Pennsylvania College of Pharmacy and Dave worked as an audio engineer in a recording studio.

All this time they had been doing nothing to prevent pregnancy and the "kid thing" still hadn't happened. Though they continued to leave it "in God's hands," they became more intentional about trying to become pregnant. It didn't work so, as Amy was nearing the end of her pharmacy program, they decided to go into infertility treatment. Amy graduated in 2006 with a doctoral degree in pharmacy and a diagnosis of undiagnosed infertility.

Dave and Amy found themselves in a Crock-Pot.

Amy describes her time in a Crock-Pot as a "very dark" time that she tries to "glaze over." She stated that she felt like "a failure" because her body "wasn't doing what it was supposed to do." She also stated that she "knew it was a God thing" because the infertility doctors could find no reason why they weren't getting pregnant, and she was consequently "angry at God" for "withholding" children from them. She went on to talk about how powerless she felt and how unfamiliar this feeling was to her. She described both herself and Dave as "go-getters" who "make things happen" that they want. Their inability to "make this happen" was very difficult for her.

Dave describes his time in the Crock-Pot as "pretty tough." He stated he felt angry and depressed and wondered why it was "so easy" for others to get pregnant and "so hard" for them. He handled his thoughts and feelings by doing "a lot of emotional eating" and subsequently "gained a lot of weight." He further stated that they both did a lot of spending in an effort to "comfort" themselves.

Amy eventually got to "the end of" herself where she "could not do one more medical test" and was "pretty clear what the next step was," i.e. adoption. Dave however, was "not there." He wanted his own biological child. Amy was done trying to make this happen and was ready to adopt. For her, it then became a matter of "getting him up to speed." She accomplished this with "a lot of prayer." God then worked through a man in their small group who told them that he had been adopted and shared his story with them. This was "a turning point" for Dave, and he became willing to adopt.

God did not take them out of the Crock-Pot for a while though.

They began the adoption process and were pretty quickly matched with "baby Christopher." They spent three hours in the hospital with Christopher and "loved him." They thought the adoption was "a done deal." Then, as they were getting ready to take Christopher home, Christopher's biological father came forward and petitioned for custody and the rug was pulled out from under Dave and Amy. It was very quickly replaced with another rug though. Later that very same day, they met Patricia, whom Dave described as "a kindred spirit." After Patricia got to know them, she decided that she wanted to give them her baby. The father was out of the picture. He had washed his hands of the baby, so this was not going to be an issue. Patricia let Dave and Amy name the baby and let them be present in the delivery room with her. They took Josiah home when he was discharged from the hospital. This was in February 2008. Dave and Amy felt blessed and grateful to God for providing them with an avenue to have a family and immediately "got busy with a second adoption." The adoption paperwork was completed, in the folder and ready to submit when they found out Amy was pregnant. Josiah was four months old at that point.

One would think the news of the pregnancy would fill Dave and Amy with much joy. It didn't. It filled each of them with many mixed thoughts and feelings. Dave's initial reaction to the pregnancy was to feel "jerked around, upset, and confused" as he had "closed the door" on having his own biological child. He felt like a "still fresh wound" was being "reopened." Amy was initially in denial, sure that the result of the pregnancy test was a false positive. She stated that once she finally believed that she really was pregnant, she had trouble enjoying the pregnancy because she "kept waiting for the other shoe to drop." In addition, each of them had come to believe that they were "called into adoption" and were completely at a loss to understand what God was up to. Amy's other shoe never did drop and in December

'08 she gave birth to their daughter, Annie, *and* Josiah's adoption was finalized. So, after spending nine years trying to have a family, within the space of ten months, they found themselves the parents of two children both under the age of one year.

Though God blessed Dave and Amy with both an adoptive child and a biological child, he did not make it easy on them. Amy's pregnancy was a high-risk pregnancy which resulted in Annie being born two months early. Annie was then admitted to a neonatal intensive care unit. Throughout the following four weeks Amy felt "torn" between two babies who needed her. She was constantly juggling trips to the hospital to visit Annie with time spent at home with Josiah. Annie was finally discharged, and they brought her home to join their family. One would think this would be the end of the story. It's not.

One year later, Amy got pregnant again. Once again, God blessed them and once again he did not make it easy on them. This was also a high risk pregnancy; however, it had a different twist. When Amy was thirteen weeks pregnant, Dave and Amy saw two babies on an ultrasound and heard two heartbeats. They later found out that one baby was fine and one baby was not. One of the babies did not survive the pregnancy. The other did and in September '10, Amy gave birth to their son, Asher. He was also born two months early and also spent time in a neonatal intensive care unit before joining their family when he was six weeks old. This is the end of the story, for now.

As Amy reflected on their journey to become a family—in particular, the time she spent simmering in a Crock-Pot—she spoke about how hard it was for her to accept the reality that she is not in control of her life and to accept that God is actually the one who is in control of her life. Though the time she spent waiting on God was long and difficult and painful, the deep trust she developed in God as a result of this is now the priceless treasure which is the foundation of her life. Dave also learned to trust God on a deeper level as a result of their journey to become a family. He stated that this experience "reiterated" to him that God is truly in control of his life and he has been able to "rest in that fact."

At the time of this writing, all three children are happy and healthy. Dave moved out of the recording industry and is serving as a full-time worship pastor in a church near their home, and Amy is working part-time as a pharmacist. Each one is doing what he/she was created to do. They finally have the family they both yearned for as well as an explanation as to why it was so difficult for them to get pregnant. Following Asher's delivery, the doctor was able to put the medical pieces together and explain to them why they were infertile, why Amy's pregnancies were high-risk, and why the babies were born prematurely. The same condition caused each of these scenarios.

Amy and Dave, as well as each of the twenty-first century waiters and biblical waiters discussed in this book, had long, frustrating, confusing, painful, heartbreaking periods of time in which they waited on

God. Each one remained faithful to God during these times and continued to trust that he had a plan for his or her life. God rewarded their faithfulness and trust in him by blessing them beyond their wildest dreams. He will do the same for each of us who wait on him in trust and obedience. To God be the glory!

Consequences of Refusing to Wait on God

When you throw a stone into a pond, ripples go out from where the stone landed, and sometimes, it's hard to pinpoint exactly where the ripples stop. It's the same way with every choice we make and every action we take or refuse to take. Everything we do or do not do has consequences and those consequences are inescapable. We may escape the consequences in the short run; however, in the long run someone will experience those consequences—either us or someone who comes after us. The same holds true for waiting on God. There are consequences to waiting on God and there are consequences to refusing to wait on God. The Apostle Paul told the church in Galatia and us, "You will always harvest what you plant" (Galatians 6:7). Isaac Newton told us, "For every action, there is an equal and opposite reaction."

One example of this principle is what happened to David, Bathsheba, and David's children when David refused to live according to God's standards. Another and more dramatic example of consequences that resulted when two individuals refused to wait on God is what happened to Old Testament patriarch Abraham and his wife Sarah and all their descendants.

As stated in chapter 2, God created a people who were set apart to belong to him, to be his family, and he chose Abraham to be the father of his family. Abraham's name at birth was Abram and Sarah's name at birth was Sarai. The Bible tells us, "Sarai was unable to become pregnant and had no children" (Genesis 11:30).

Abram and Sarai were living with Abram's father in Haran when God spoke to Abram.

> The Lord had said to Abram, "Leave your native country, your relatives, and your father's family, and go to the land that I will show you. I will make you into a great nation. I will bless you and make you famous, and you will be a blessing to others." So Abram departed as the Lord had instructed…Abram was seventy-five years old when he left Haran. He took his wife, Sarai, his nephew, Lot, and all his wealth… and headed for the land of Canaan. When they arrived in Canaan… the Lord appeared to Abram and said, "I will give this land to your descendants."
>
> Genesis 12:1–2, 4–5

Note: Abram had no descendants.

When Doing Isn't Enough

A number of years later, the Lord once again verbalized his promise to Abram.

> So Abram settled in the land of Canaan... the Lord said to Abram, "Look as far as you can see in every direction—north and south, east and west. I am giving all this land, as far as you can see, to you and your descendants as a permanent possession. And I will give you so many descendants that, like the dust of the earth, they cannot be counted!"
>
> Genesis 13:12, 14–16

Note: Abram still had no descendants.

> Some time later, the Lord spoke to Abram in a vision and said to him, "Do not be afraid, Abram, for I will protect you, and your reward will be great." But Abram replied, "O Sovereign Lord, what good are all your blessings when I don't even have a son? Since you've given me no children, Eliezer of Damascus, a servant in my household, will inherit all my wealth. You have given me no descendants of my own, so one of my servants will be my heir." Then the Lord said to him, "No, your servant will not be your heir, for you will have a son of your own who will be your heir." Then the Lord took Abram outside and said to him, "Look up into the sky and count the stars if you can. That's how many descendants you will have!" And Abram believed the Lord, and the Lord counted him as righteous because of his faith.
>
> Genesis 15:1–6

So the Lord made a covenant with Abram that day and said, "I have given this land to your descendants, all the way from the border of Egypt to the great Euphrates River".

Genesis 15:18

Now Sarai, Abram's wife, had not been able to bear children for him. But she had an Egyptian servant named Hagar. So Sarai said to Abram "The Lord has prevented me from having children. Go and sleep with my servant. Perhaps I can have children through her." And Abram agreed with Sarai's proposal. So Sarai, Abram's wife, took Hagar the Egyptian servant and gave her to Abram as a wife. (This happened ten years after Abram had settled in the land of Canaan.) So Abram had sexual relations with Hagar, and she became pregnant...

So Hagar gave Abram a son, and Abram named him Ishmael. Abram was eighty-six years old when Ishmael was born.

Genesis 16:1–4, 15–16

Sarai grew tired of waiting on God to do what he said he was going to do, so she devised a plan to try to make it happen herself. Abram agreed with her and went along with her plan. The catch was that Abram and Sarai's plan did not match God's plan.

> When Abram was ninety-nine years old, the Lord appeared to him and said, "I am El-Shaddai—God Almighty. Serve me faithfully and live a blameless life. I will make a covenant with you, by which I will guarantee to

give you countless descendants." At this, Abram fell face down on the ground. Then God said to him, "This is my covenant with you: I will make you the father of a multitude of nations! What's more, I am changing your name. It will no longer be Abram. Instead, you will be called Abraham, for you will be the father of many nations. I will make you extremely fruitful. Your descendants will become many nations, and kings will be among them! I will confirm my covenant with you and your descendants after you, from generation to generation. This is the everlasting covenant: I will always be your God and the God of your descendants after you. And I will give the entire land of Canaan, where you now live as a foreigner, to you and your descendants. It will be their possession forever, and I will be their God."

Genesis 17:1–8

Then God said to Abraham, "Regarding Sarai, your wife—her name will no longer be Sarai. From now on her name will be Sarah. And I will bless her and give you a son from her! Yes, I will bless her richly, and she will become the mother of many nations. Kings of nations will be among her descendants." Then Abraham bowed down to the ground, but he laughed to himself in disbelief. "How could I become a father at the age of 100?" he thought. "And how can Sarah have a baby when she is ninety years old?" So Abraham said to God, "May Ishmael live under your special blessing!" But God replied, "No, Sarah, your wife, will give birth to a son for you. You will name him Isaac, and I will confirm my covenant with him and his descendants as an everlasting covenant. As for Ishmael, I will bless him also, just as you have asked. I will make him extremely fruitful and multiply his descendants. He will become the father of twelve princes, and I will make him a great nation. But my covenant will be confirmed with Isaac, who will be born to you and Sarah about this time next year."

Genesis 17:15–21

"The Lord kept his word and did for Sarah exactly what he had promised. She became pregnant, and she gave birth to a son for Abraham in his old age. This happened at just the time God had said it would. And Abraham named their son Isaac" (Genesis 21:1–3). Later, when the two boys had grown up, God said to Abraham, "Isaac is the son through whom your descendants will be counted. But I will also make a nation of the descendants of Hagar's son because he is your son, too" (Genesis 21:12–13).

Ishmael became the father of the Arab nation. Abraham, through Isaac, is the father of the nation of Israel. Both nations have laid claim to the Promised Land as both are descendants of Abraham. Much Arab blood and much Israeli blood has been spilled in the conflict between the two nations over the ownership of the land from the border of Egypt to the Euphrates River. "Contrary to the Jewish claim that this land was promised only to the descendants of Abraham's younger son Isaac, they (Arabs) argue that the Land of Canaan was promised to what they consider the elder son, Ishmael, from whom Arabs claim descent" (Wikipedia).

Arab-Israeli Conflict

There has been tension and conflict between the Arabs and the Jews and between each of them and the British forces ever since the 1917 Balfour Declaration and the 1920 creation of the British Mandate of Palestine. Both the Arabs and the Jews were dissatisfied with British policies. The Arab opposition developed into the 1936–1939 Arab revolt in Palestine. The Jewish resistance developed into the Jewish insurgency in Palestine. These ongoing tensions erupted on November 30, 1947, into the civil war between the Arab and Jewish populations in response to the UN Partition Plan to divide Palestine into an Arab state, a Jewish state, and the Special International Regime for the City of Jerusalem. On May 14, 1948, the British Mandate of Palestine expired, and the modern State of Israel was established. On that day military forces from Egypt, Jordan, and Syria, together with expeditionary forces from Iraq, invaded Palestine. They took control of the Arab areas and immediately attacked Israeli forces and several Jewish settlements. The ten months of fighting separated by several truce periods took place mostly on the former territory of the British Mandate and for a short time also in the Sinai Peninsula and southern Lebanon. This conflict ended in 1949 with the signing of the 1949 Armistice Agreements between Israel and each of its Arab neighbors.

Casualties

Israel lost 6,373 of its people, about 1 percent of its population at the time, in this war. About 4,000 were soldiers and the rest were civilians. Around 2,000 were Holocaust survivors.

The exact number of Arab casualties is unknown. One estimate places the Arab death toll at 7,000, including 3,000 Palestinians, 2,000 Egyptians, 1,000 Jordanians, and 1,000 Syrians. According to Henry Laurens, the Palestinians suffered double the Jewish losses, with 13,000 dead, 1,953 of whom are known to have died in combat situations. Of the remainder, 4,004 remain nameless but the place, tally, and date of their death is known, and a further 7,043, for whom only the place of death is known, not their identities nor the date of their death. According to Laurens, the largest part of Palestinian casualties consisted of non-combatants and corresponds to the successful operations of the Israelis.

The 1948 war between the Arabs and the Israelis also resulted in approximately 711,000 Palestinian refugees who fled or were expelled from the area that became Israel. They were not allowed to return to their homes. They ended up in refugee camps in surrounding countries, including Lebanon, Jordan, Syria, and the area that was later to be known as the Gaza Strip. Approximately 400 Arab towns and villages were depopulated during the 1948 Palestinian exodus.

The war and the creation of the State of Israel also triggered the Jewish exodus from Arab lands. In the three years following the war, about 700,000 Jews residing elsewhere in the Middle East fled or were expelled from their countries, with many of those Jewish refugees migrating to Israel.

Since the establishment of the State of Israel in 1948, Arabs and Israelis have engaged in seven major wars and a number of minor conflicts. Two major Palestinian intifadas (uprisings) have also occurred. The wars include the 1956 Suez War; 1967 Six-Day War; the War of Attrition, a limited war fought between Egypt and Israel from 1967 to 1970; the 1973 Yom Kippur War; the 1982 First Lebanon War; the 2006 Second Lebanon War; and the 2008–2009 Gaza War.

Casualties

The seven wars between the Arabs and the Israelis resulted in more than 6,000 Israeli military casualties and more than 26,000 Arab military casualties, to say nothing of the thousands of military personnel that were wounded and the thousands of Israeli and Arab civilians that were killed or wounded. In addition to the military casualties resulting from the wars, thousands of Israeli soldiers and Arab soldiers have been killed in miscellaneous engagements and terrorist attacks while more than 3,000 Israeli civilians have been killed and 25,000 have been wounded and an unknown number of Arab civilians have been killed or wounded since the establishment of the state of Israel in 1948 until today.

(All information regarding the Arab Israeli conflict was taken from Wikipedia.)

Thought to Ponder

It's mindboggling to think that this might all have been averted if only Sarah and Abraham had trusted God enough to wait on him.

Though the consequences you and I (or our descendants) may experience for refusing to wait on God will most probably not be as devastating or as far-reaching as those Abraham and Sarah and their descendants experienced, there will still be consequences nonetheless. On the other hand, if we choose to wait on God, the benefits of waiting make the wait worthwhile.

Benefits of Waiting on God

"I have promised many blessings to those who wait on Me: *renewed strength*, living above one's circumstances, resurgence of hope, awareness of My continual Presence. Waiting on Me enables you to glorify Me by living in deep dependence on Me, ready to do My will. It also helps you to enjoy Me; *in my Presence is fullness of Joy*."[1]

As stated in chapter 4, in September 2013, I left the Brethren in Christ Church where I had been leading the Celebrate Recovery ministry. I returned for a special event in February 2014. While I was there God let me know in no uncertain terms that he wanted me in that church body, not in the new congregation I had been attending. So, I went back to the Brethren in Christ Church and have been attending that church ever since. God has not revealed to me yet why he wants me there; however, he has rewarded my obedience by blessing me with an abundance of the internal peace and joy that I treasure so much. In the meantime, I'm still in the

Crock-Pot. Since God has not yet ended my season of waiting, I am assuming that there is more simmering I need to do, more lessons I need to learn.

As also stated in chapter 4, God has been leading me and guiding me since I gave my life to him in the mid-1990s. There have been times he called me to action, and there have been times he has instructed me to wait. God used the times of waiting to develop my character. I was not a passive participant in this process though; I was a very active participant. It was a cooperative process, a joint effort. My part in the process involved the choices I made while I was in the Crock-Pot regarding how I reacted to and handled myself during the waiting/simmering time.

Planting Fruit and Gifts

When we decide to become part of God's family by giving our life to him and submitting to his will for us, the Holy Spirit takes up residence inside us. When the Holy Spirit comes to live inside a believer, he plants fruit in that individual and endows him or her with spiritual gifts.

The Apostle Paul described the fruit the Holy Spirit plants inside us in his letter to the church in Galatia. "The Holy Spirit produces this kind of fruit in our lives: love, joy, peace, patience, kindness, goodness, faithfulness, gentleness, and self-control" (Galatians 5:22).

Paul discussed spiritual gifts in his first letter to the church in Corinth. A spiritual gift is an ability or talent that is given to an individual by God to equip him or her to fulfill the purpose God chose for that individual.

> A spiritual gift is given to each of us so we can help each other. To one person the Spirit gives the ability to give wise advice; to another the same Spirit gives a message of special knowledge. The same Spirit gives great faith to another, and to someone else the one Spirit gives the gift of healing. He gives one person the power to perform miracles, and another the ability to prophesy. He gives someone else the ability to discern whether a message is from the Spirit of God or from another spirit. Still another person is given the ability to speak in unknown languages, while another is given the ability to interpret what is being said. It is the one and only Spirit who distributes all these gifts. He alone decides which gift each person should have.
>
> 1 Corinthians 12:7–11

Paul also spoke about spiritual gifts in his letter to the church in Ephesus and his letter to the church in Rome. "He has given each one of us a special gift through the generosity of Christ" (Ephesians 4:7).

> In his grace, God has given us different gifts for doing certain things well. So if God has given you the ability to prophesy, speak out with as much faith as God has given you. If your gift is serving others, serve them well. If you are a teacher, teach well. If your gift is to encourage others, be encouraging. If it is giving, give

generously. If God has given you leadership ability, take the responsibility seriously. And if you have a gift for showing kindness to others, do it gladly.

Romans 12:6–9

Growing Fruit and Gifts

Though the fruit of the Spirit and our spiritual gifts are planted in us when we become children of God, they are in seed form at that time. They need to grow and develop. Though there are many avenues that God can use to develop the fruit and our gifts, I believe that one of the most powerful ways he grows them is by having us go through seasons of waiting or placing us in a Crock-Pot. He certainly has used those methods with me!

In addition to teaching me, during my first time in the divine Crock-Pot (2004–2006), that my source of self-esteem and self-worth is not in my professional work or in my ministry, he also taught me how to forgive. During that time, I was healing from a very deep emotional wound. My healing process moved along in fits and starts. I experienced victories followed by relapses. As this happened repeatedly, I gradually came to understand that God had allowed this hurtful incident to happen to me in order to teach me how to forgive. He slowly and convincingly revealed my spirit of unforgiveness to me, and I came to see that my life was not characterized by forgiveness, as Jesus wants his followers' lives to be. Rather, my life was characterized by holding grudges and harboring bitterness, resentment, and a desire for vengeance. Though I knew that forgiveness is at the heart of the gospel message and I had received God's forgiveness for my sins when I accepted Jesus's work on the cross, I was not extending forgiveness to others who wronged or hurt me. God showed me that I was not walking out this vital part of the Christian walk. He further showed me that my spirit of unforgiveness would stop me from fulfilling my destiny.

As I struggled to forgive the individuals who had hurt me, I fought against my desire to get back at them, to make them hurt as much as they had hurt me. I quickly realized that I could not forgive them on my own. My desire for vengeance was too strong. I needed God's help, his power. I began to daily ask God to give me an attitude and lifestyle of forgiveness. I simultaneously made a decision that I was no longer going to allow them to steal my joy. As I daily prayed this prayer and reiterated my decision, my peace and joy slowly came back and God finally took me out of the divine Crock-Pot.

When I exited the Crock-Pot, my relationship with God was substantially strengthened, particularly my dependence on him.

My second time in the divine Crock-Pot (September 2013 to the present) seems to have some of the same purposes as the first time. God is continuing to chisel away at my need to garner approval from human beings and draw worth from what I *do* rather than who I *am*. Don't just do something, stand there! As a task-oriented overachiever living in a culture that values achievement and sees waiting as something to be avoided if possible, this often leaves me feeling uncomfortable and insecure. When I find myself wallowing in those feelings, I consciously remind myself that I am living my life for an audience of One and that what human beings think about me or say about me is irrelevant.

Choices

In summary, while we're waiting or simmering, there are many choices we need to make. It is the choices we make that determine to what extent spiritual fruit will grow in us and our gifts will be developed. For example, we can choose to sink into despair or we can choose to wait in expectant hope. We can choose to be patient (regardless of how we feel) or we can choose to be impatient and irritable and drive ourselves and people around us crazy. We can choose to allow God to do a course correction or we can continue on a path of our own choosing. We can persevere in the time of waiting until God brings it to an end or we can take matters into our own hands and end it ourselves.

When we wait in expectant hope and allow God to do a course correction and/or persevere in the time of waiting, the fruits of faithfulness and self-control grow. When we choose to be patient, the fruit of patience (obviously) grows. When we abide by God's will and timing, we experience the peace and joy that surpasses human understanding. When we are filled with the peace and joy that only God can give, we naturally manifest behavior which is marked by love, kindness, goodness, and gentleness.

My Choice

I am choosing to believe that God is not finished with me yet, that there is more he wants me to do for him and for his kingdom. I further believe that God put me in this season of waiting to prepare me for whatever it is he has in store for me next. I am choosing to believe the old adage: "*Good things come to those who wait.*" I am ending this book the same way I began it—in this time of uncertainty, I am waiting and trusting, praising him in the hallway.

Afterword

Not all of us were fortunate enough to grow up with Christian parents who modeled a personal faith in Christ right before our eyes. I didn't. Therefore, getting to know the real God and learning to trust him and surrendering to him was a struggle for me. If this is true for you as well, I suggest you work a 12 Step program.

It was through working the 12 Steps with Jesus Christ as my Higher Power that I learned how to trust God, how to surrender to him, how to obey him, and how to wait on him. I also developed clarity regarding what I can control and what I cannot control.

Though the 12 Steps were developed by Bill W. and Dr. Bob as a roadmap or path to recovery when they founded Alcoholics Anonymous in the 1930s, the 12 Steps are not only applicable to drug and/or alcohol problems. They are applicable to any struggle in life, including difficulty trusting God.

Interestingly enough, many people believe that the 12 Steps were divinely inspired, and indeed, Bill W. founded Alcoholics Anonymous following a spiritual experience he had in which his desire to drink alcohol was removed. For me, the 12 Steps have proven to be a roadmap to God and guidelines for living a Christian life.

Step 1: *We admitted we were powerless over our addictions and compulsive behaviors, that our lives had become unmanageable* is an invitation to face reality and admit that our life isn't working with us in control. We stop pretending that it is working, we admit our powerlessness and stop trying to manage our life our way.

Step 1, if worked properly, leaves us feeling empty and ready for Step 2: *We came to believe that a power greater than ourselves could restore us to sanity.* When we begin to see that help is available to us, and as we reach out and accept what our Higher Power has to offer, we start to feel hopeful that our life will improve and we'll feel better. To take this step, we need not understand what lies ahead. We need to trust that God knows what lies ahead and that he loves us and will take care of us. In Brian's words "God's got it".

Taking Step 2 positions us to take Step 3: *We made a decision to turn our lives and our wills over to the care of God*. In the first two steps, we became aware of our condition and accepted the idea of a power greater than ourselves. Step 3 is decision time. When we take Step 3, God becomes the manager of our life and we learn to accept life on his terms.

We may have been taught to believe that we only have to accept Christ as our Lord and Savior for our lives to be complete and satisfying. Our proclamation that "I am a born-again Christian; my past is washed clean; I am a new creature; Christ has totally changed me" is true. Our Spirits are born again. Our flesh, however, is not. Our flesh has lived in the world and is bearing consequences of that. We are most probably carrying around buried unhealed hurts, engaging in some maladaptive habits, and holding onto some destructive hang-ups. In order to truly live the life Jesus died to give us, we need more than salvation. We need transformation. Working the additional nine steps with Jesus Christ as our Higher Power (doing and sharing an inventory of our lives, making amends to people we have hurt, forgiving people who have hurt us, praying and taking an inventory daily, helping others) can and will lead to transformation. I can tell you from personal experience that it will enrich your personal relationship with God and enable you to wait on him if you choose to do so.

Notes

Introduction

1. Henry T. Blackaby & Claude V. King, *Experiencing God* (Nashville, Tennessee: LifeWay Press, 1990) p. 18
2. John Maxwell, *A Leader's Heart* (Nashville, Tennessee: Thomas Nelson, 2010) p. 232
3. Sarah Young, *Jesus Calling* (Nashville, Tennessee: Thomas Nelson, 2004) p. 89

Waiting

1. Ibid., p. 362

Knowing

1. Henry T. Blackaby & Claude V. King, *Experiencing God* (Nashville, Tennessee: LifeWay Press, 1990) p. 42

Obedience: The Critical Ingredient

1. Ibid., p. 146
2. Ibid., p. 147

Benefits of Waiting on God

1. Sarah Young, *Jesus Calling* (Nashville, Tennessee: Thomas Nelson, 2004) p. 89

www.ingramcontent.com/pod-product-compliance
Lightning Source LLC
LaVergne TN
LVHW051501070426
835507LV00022B/2876